ROUGHING IT EASY 2

WARNER BOOKS

A Warner Communications Company

ROUGHING IT EASY 2

Dian Thomas

WARNER BOOKS EDITION

Copyright © 1977 by Dian Thomas
All rights reserved

ISBN 0-446-87430-2
Warner Books, Inc., 75 Rockefeller Plaza, New York, N.Y. 10019

A Warner Communications Company

Printed in the United States of America
Not associated with Warner Press, Inc. of Anderson, Indiana
First Printing: June, 1977

10 9 8 7 6 5 4 3 2 1

To my brothers (who are great outdoorsmen):
Neal
Jay
Jared
Clyde

CONTENTS

FOREWORD

To top the success and quality of her first book, *Roughing It Easy,* seems an almost impossible task, but Dian Thomas has done it and done it beautifully!

She has taken the cooking and camping conveniences of civilization and imaginatively adapted them for outdoor use. There are recipes to tempt an epicure and camping techniques to ease one's way to the farthest horizons. She has given a fine guide to both family camping amateurs and wilderness camping experts.

The new skill of solar cookery is described in *Roughing It Easy II,* and the old skill of home drying of trail and camp foods is modernized.

In this day of diminishing resources and expanding use of the outdoors, Dian's creative recycling approach is timely, in addition to being fun!

The recipe for this book? Expertise and experience, plus a pinch of humor and a dash of freshness and a very tasty seasoning of fun and adventure!

Wood smoke and the rich smell of good cookery rise right out of these pages!

Ernest F. Schmidt
Executive Vice-President of
American Camping Association (Retired)
Director of Camping
National Training Center
Boy Scouts of America (Retired)
Member of Explorers Club

PREFACE

Nature beckons to us all. To experience the adventure of being on our own in the glorious outdoors is an urge few can resist at one time or another in their lives. We need to get away from the hurry-scurry of today's world—horns honking, cars screeching, time schedules, smog-filled skies, structured daily activities—away to the quiet natural surrounding of wilderness. We need to be free from pressing schedules, to rise with the sun rather than a buzzing alarm, to be where our time is all our own. We need to breathe fresh air and drink pure water, to exercise our ingenuity and imagination in order to live with nature and enjoy the seasons of the year.

This book is written to help make that pursuit easier—more enjoyable and inexpensive. The emphasis is on using your own ability and imagination rather than your pocketbook, whether you plan to camp with a station wagon full of family or hike into the wilderness alone, for a weekend or for a week-long retreat.

ACKNOWLEDGMENTS

It is with gratitude that I recognize the skills and expertise of others who helped produce this book.

Thanks go to Dave Neilson for his assistance and research in preparing this manuscript; to Deanna DeLong for her excellent work on the lightweight camping section; to John Haek for his work on the backpacks and lightweight stoves; to Louise G. Hanson for her research and editorial work; to Dianne T. King for typing the manuscript; and to Stan Macbean for the photographs and Ralph Reynolds for the line drawings. I am grateful for the contribution of each one of them.

Others, for lending their support and good will, have my deepest thanks; they are Rita Singer, Sandy Watrous, Donna and Kriket Neilson, Arthur J. Kirkham, and Lee Armstrong.

I am indebted to D. S. Halacy, Jr., for his sections on "make-it-yourself solar cooking" in this book, taken originally from his *Fun with the Sun,* now in *Experiments with Solar Energy.* He has also allowed us to use his detailed plans (from the same book) for making a water heater to be used in camping. For these exciting do-it-yourself sections, we not only thank him—we salute him!

INTRODUCTION

What's your favorite season?

It's spring, you say—when that familiar urge to become a part of nature hits you? The hills surrounding your valley are greening; a chipmunk flits from behind a rock, runs across a clearing, and scampers up a scrub oak tree; bees light on uncurling buds; birds soar and sing; and your heart soars with them.

But then, summer is nice, too. The heat of the city turns your gaze to nature, where green trees and cool streams invite you. Shade is there, under those trees, and fish are in the streams waiting for your hook and line. And you could spend eternity there.

Or do you prefer autumn?—when you're filled with a poignant longing to see the fall colors, to dream beside a creek bed while bright leaves drop silently around you in the Indian summer goldness. The air is heavy with the odor of full, ripe things ready to be harvested. And you would catch time, if you could, and stop it—and stay there.

Perhaps your favorite season is winter? The snowpack is just right for skiing. There's a tingle in the air and excitement in your veins. The slopes are a siren, and there's no resisting their call. And you'd like to spend weeks in the snow!

No matter your choice of the seasons, you need the know-how to get out into nature and stay there as long as you'd like. Do you know how to live with ease in the out-of-doors? What should you take with you on a summer's outing for a week (or longer) of relaxed living? How could you stand the crisp autumn nights, or the chilling cold of winter?

Good news! You can take your pick—spring, summer, fall, or winter—and take your trip into nature. Whatever the season, you can weather it; there's help for you in the chapters that follow.

An equipment chapter, for example, offers some suggestions to launch you on a creative, inexpensive spree. No need to spend a fortune on gear. Make some of it yourself; you'll enjoy it more, and you'll take pride in the work of your own hands.

Do you want to know about the kinds of shelters you should take with you, whether for backpacking or family camping—for good weather or bad? There are answers for that, too—and how to select a good site and take care of your shelter.

Another chapter will tell you how to keep toasty in cold weather, day or night. It will tell you something about your body metabolism, about clothing you should wear, and about types of sleeping bags for various occasions.

And when you've learned about equipment and camping, you can learn some basic cooking principles that will help you create new methods of cooking on your own. Recipes are included for each cooking method. Again, you'll want to think up some recipes yourself.

Lightweight camping will be discussed, including how to dry fruits and vegetables, how to choose the right kind of backpack, and how to choose a lightweight stove.

You will even find sections on the latest thing in camping—solar heating and cooking.

Remember, too, that nature provides its own rules and is full of pleasant surprises that will encourage your creativity. Be sure, of course, that you help her remain a pleasant hostess. Where the cooking methods call for sticks for cooking, use fallen branches or twigs whenever possible instead of green ones cut from trees. Be familiar with local shrubs and trees. Some are poisonous. Be particularly aware of the ecology and resources of the area, and treat it accordingly.

Whatever season you choose, enjoy a vacation secure in the knowledge that you know what you're doing. You will return to your job and your daily routine relaxed—fortified with the memories of days and nights spent with nature's glorious and revitalizing spirit.

CAR CAMPING

Camping together can be a positive influence on any family. Enjoying the beauties of nature while working together to provide the daily necessities of food and shelter will help your entire family feel closer.

Car camping is practical—especially for families with younger children. Plenty of activities keep everyone busy, but if things get dull, it is easy enough to move on. With some of the practical suggestions included in the chapters that follow, you can be protected from the elements, eat well with some rather imaginative cooking methods, and still cover a lot of the scenic terrain of our beautiful country. Car camping is also necessary if you are driving a distance to your favorite backpacking spot.

EQUIPMENT

Equipment for any kind of outdoor activity comes in so many shapes and sizes that if you are like most people, you could never collect—or afford—all those "just right" and expensive trappings. You would need a fortune to buy them, a transportation fleet to carry them, and a computer system to keep everything catalogued and in order.

On the other hand, if you devise your own traveling and camping equipment, you'll be able to have all the gear you'll ever need, without great expense. Many useful items can be made or improvised from household articles. You will be surprised at what you can turn out with a few basic tools and a little know-how. Although the results may not qualify for a beautiful-design contest, the equipment will be functional, and that is the most important requirement.

The goal of this chapter is to help you experience the thrill that can come from creating your own equipment and adapting it to your personal uses.

PERSONAL EQUIPMENT

It's hard to escape housekeeping and personal grooming, even if you are camping or traveling, but you can make it easy and fun if you set your creative talents free to work for you. All you need are a few ideas to help you get started. Here are some starting points to spur on your imagination.

Laundry

Camping or traveling can be made more enjoyable if you can slip into a change of clothes, freshly washed, when you begin to feel "grubby." Have fun with these "washers," then devise one of your own, if you feel so inclined.

Agitating washer. Make a portable agitating washer with any tall, waterproof container: a clean garbage can, the 2-gallon container that ice cream is carried in (it may be either plastic or metal), or others.

- Cover the soiled clothing with water and soap, leaving space at the top for the action of the plunger.
- Using a new or a clean toilet plunger (fig. 1), agitate the clothing with up-and-down and round-and-round motions in the water.

(See also "Hot Water Supply" later in this chapter for heating water for your wash.)

Traveling washer. If you are traveling, you can do your washing in a sealed container.

- Cover the clothing with water and add soap.
- Seal and place the container in a place in your car where it will not tip over (fig. 2).

A sealed plastic garbage liner can be used if the container does not have a sealed lid. The bumpier the road, the more "heavy duty" the agitation. A smooth ride will provide only gentle agitation, and additional hand agitation may be required.

 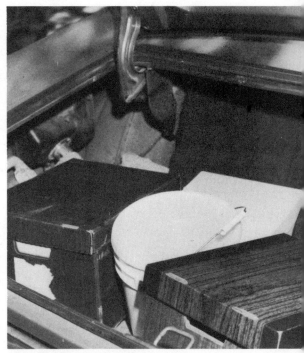

Fig.1. Agitating washer   **Fig.2. Traveling washer**

Grooming Apron

Have you had trouble finding a convenient place in camp to put your grooming items as you attempt to brush your teeth and comb your hair? Make a handy apron for toilet items, and you'll never again have to search among the rocks and dirt for a wet toothbrush and a comb covered with leaves and insects.

Take a bath towel, fold up the lower edge about 5 inches, and sew pockets for toiletry items such as toothpaste, soap, cup, comb, mirror, and washcloth. Sew a casing about 2 inches above the pockets and thread a drawstring through it, making it long enough to tie around the waist (fig. 3).

The excess material at the top can become a flap to keep the items in the pocket from falling out and can also serve as a towel for drying your hands and face (fig. 4).

Fig.3. Grooming apron

**Fig.4. Using grooming apron
as a towel**

Outdoor Shower

If you hesitate to go camping because you're afraid you'll have to do without your daily shower, fear no more. This one is quick and simple to put together. And it works beautifully (fig. 5).

- At a hardware store or insecticide outlet, buy a 2½-gallon compressed-air can or a can about that size such as you would use in your back yard. (The can has a 2-foot hose, a wand, and a handle that releases the spray and shuts it off again.)

- Unscrew the wand from the hose. (You won't need the wand again unless you decide at a future date to spray insects. You really shouldn't use the same can for both.)

- At a plumbing supply store, get a 1¼-inch f.i.p. (female iron pipe) x $^{15}/_{16}$-inch male aerator adapter. Buy a portable water sprayer (Alson's Spray, snap-on Model 250PB, or a similar portable shower head. The adapter might be a slightly different size for another brand of sprayer. Ask your plumber to help you pick out the right one.)

- Screw the aerator adapter into the end of the portable sprayer hose, then screw the end of the hose on the compressed-air can into the aerator adapter.

Using any of the means presented later in this chapter for heating water, prepare water the temperature you like for a shower and pour it into the opened compressor can. Replace the lid containing the pump handle. (*Do not place the can in coals or flame to heat the water.* The compressed air could cause the can to explode if the water should become too hot.)

- Pump up the pressure in the can with the pump handle. Press down the water handle on the hose to release the water; then press down the clamp next to the handle to keep the water flowing.

- Release the water at the shower head by pressing the button on the side. You may turn the water on and off here as you take your shower.

- Give the compressor can a few more pumps if necessary to keep the water flowing.

- You could tie the shower head to a tree limb. Tie black plastic around the shower, and you'll have a private place to shower. A portable floor could also be constructed with boards. Cut two 2x4's about 3 feet long. Lay them 2 feet apart, and place additonal boards across, leaving about 1 inch of space so water can run through. Nail in place.

And there you have it. It's a shower just like yours at home—

Fig.5. Outdoor shower

without the trimmings—but it's even more enjoyable when you're roughing it.

If you want a less effective spray, use the wand instead of the shower head. The spray is much smaller, but so is the effort that you expend to make the shower.

Waste Removal

One of the obligations of a camper or a hiker is to see to proper waste removal. It is for your own protection as well as that of others. No camper should have to be reminded about the dangers of leaving human waste where flies and other insects can have access to it—to carry away and infect others with disease germs. Nor of the unpleasant odor it emanates. Following is a method for disposing of waste easily where outdoor facilities are not available.

Cat hole. As a result of our country's ecology campaign of recent years, outdoor people who have been evaluating methods and procedures recommend the following method of disposing of human waste in the out-of-doors.

- Dig a hole 6 to 8 inches deep at least 100 feet from any stream in a secluded spot.
- Use white toilet tissue, since it decomposes better than colored.
- After using the hole, cover it with dirt, as a cat does.
- Mark the spot by crossing two sticks or with a rock so that neither you nor others in your camping party will dig in the same place again.
- Leave the area as natural-looking as possible.

A second suggestion (keeping toilet tissue waterproof) is included here for the sake of comfort and convenience—a way to rough it just a little easier.

Weatherproof toilet tissue. Put your roll of toilet tissue in a weatherproof can. Here's how you can do it, using a clothes hanger and an empty, medium-sized shortening can with a plastic lid.

- With tin snips, cut a ½-inch strip the full length of the can (fig. 6). Throw away the strip.
- In the closed end of the can, about 4½ inches from the slit and as near the edge of the closed end as possible, punch a hole large enough to insert the end of a wire clothes hanger (fig. 7).
- Punch a similar hole in the plastic lid near the edge, taking care not to damage the edge.
- Measure the horizontal part of a lightweight clothes hanger the length of the can and cut it. Repeat on the other side (fig. 8). Slip one end of the cut wire through the hole in the plastic lid, the other end through the hole in the bottom of the can (fig. 9). Overlap the wires inside the can (nearly the length of the can). Tape the ends of the wires to the inside of the can with a strong tape.
- Using the tape, cover the raw edges of the slit in the can (fig. 10).
- Insert a roll of toilet tissue into the can through the open end and feed out the end of it through the slit.
- Fit the plastic lid over the open end of the can to hold it firmly together.

The coat hanger serves as a handle for carrying the tissue holder as well as a hook for hanging it on a convenient branch of a tree (fig. 11).

Fig.6. Cutting out strip

Fig.7. Punching hole with nail

Fig.8. Measuring and cutting
coat hanger

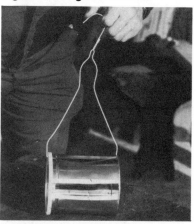

Fig.9. Placing coat hanger
through can

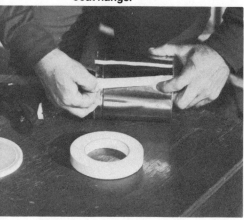

Fig.10. Taping edges of can

Fig.11. Waterproof toilet-tissues
container

25

CREATIVE GENERAL EQUIPMENT

Equipment needs vary from person to person. Yours will be different from anyone else's. For that reason, a few suggestions for general equipment are included here as a starting point for you to think up your own creations. What are your needs beyond a supply of hot water and some kitchen equipment? Give the answer some thought. You might surprise yourself with the ideas you think of.

Hot Water Supply

A part of enjoying the out-of-doors, for some people, is having an adequate supply of hot water for doing dishes, washing clothes, or bathing. The first method of heating water described here is more for a long-term camp than for a brief stay. The speed with which it will supply you with hot water will surprise you, depending, of course, on several things: the size of the water container, the heat of the fire, and particularly, the size of the coil in the fire (fig. 12).

Remember that this method of heating water can be used at home in a fireplace in case of emergency (fig. 13).

If you can buy copper tubing (⅜-inch or ½-inch) from a junk dealer, it will be much less expensive than buying it new. The garbage can you use should be galvanized, with all seams well soldered—even if you have to solder them yourself (figs. 14 and 15). Any good method of soldering, such as butane and acetylene, may be used. Test first for leaks by filling the can with water.

Fig.12. Garbage can water heater

Fig.13. Using water heater in fireplace

Fig.14. Soldering with acetylene torch

Fig.15. Soldering with butane torch

27

Fig.16. Holes to receive fittings

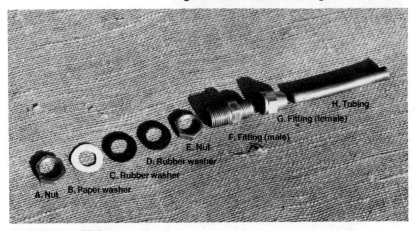

Fig.17. Parts of fitting

Copper-tubing/garbage-can water heater. Here are instructions for a whiz of a hot-water heater for your permanent camp:

■ Your ⅜-inch to ½-inch copper tubing should be approximately 13½ feet long.

■ About one inch from the bottom of the galavanized garbage can, drill or cut a hole the size to receive the fitting for the copper tubing.

■ About eight inches above the first hole, drill another one to receive the other fitting for the copper tubing (fig. 16).

■ The following parts, listed in the order of assembly, are used in placing the fittings into the can (fig. 17). It is necessary to tighten the nut (E) on the fitting (F) before inserting the fitting into the hole.

28

Fig.18. Coiling copper tubing

- Insert the fitting into the hole (from the outside of the can).
- Add the rubber washer (C) next, then the cardboard washer you've cut out of a piece of poster paper (B). (It is the same size as the rubber washer and will help keep the rubber washer from tearing apart when you exert the pressure necessary to tighten the last nut (A) to keep water from leaking.)
- Insert the copper tubing into the fitting (G).
- Repeat for the other end of the tubing.
- After the tubing comes through the fitting, flange it out a bit to make it seal.
- Now, coil the tubing, beginning the first coil about 10 or 12 inches from the end of the tubing. Coil the tubing twice or more around an object approximately 12 inches in diameter so that it won't kink (fig. 18). You should have a length of tubing left about the same as the other end of the tubing. (Caution: Bend the tubing a little at a time to prevent kinks.)
- Place the free end of the tubing onto the bottom fitting. Screw in tightly by using a wrench on both sides (fig. 19).
- Repeat with the other end on the upper hole (fig. 20).
- Place the garbage can near the fire, where the coils should be in or slightly above the flames or coals (fig. 21).

Then watch the water in the can get hot! The water will circulate freely through the hot coils, keeping the water hot as long as you keep the fire going. The principle at work here is this: the heat from the fire

Fig.19. Tightening fitting with wrenches

Fig.20. Attaching tubing to upper fitting

Fig.21. Coils placed into fire over coals

Fig.22. Food heating in double Zip-Lock bags

31

Fig.23. Faucet

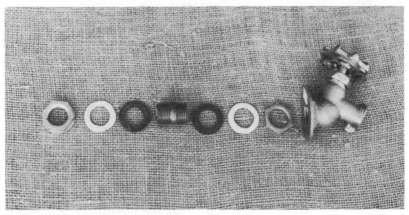

Fig.24. Fittings for attaching faucet

32

Fig.25. Coil removed and placed inside for storage and transporting

heats the cold water in the copper tubing, causing it to rise in the coils and flow back into the garbage can. As the water cools, it falls to the bottom of the can, runs into the copper tubing, and is heated again. As the cycle continues, the water will become hotter and hotter.

Try this: Fill Zip-Lock bags (for additional safety, use double bags) or Seal-a-Meal bags with food and float them in the hot water to heat. Leave the food warming in the water while you hike. When you return, your lunch will be ready. Caution: With Zip-Lock bags, remove as much air as possible before sealing (fig. 22).

For greater cleanliness and convenience, a water faucet may be inserted into the side of the can nine inches above the bottom (fig. 23). The faucet should be at least one inch above the top hole for the tubing. At this height, it will still allow the water to circulate through the coils. The same procedure is followed here as in attaching the fittings for the tubing (fig. 24).

Care should be taken in removing the coil for transporting and storage. It is best to use two wrenches so that you will not break the seal on the fitting through the side of the can. Place the coil inside the can and replace the lid (fig. 25).

Five-gallon water heater. A good way to heat water is to use a 5-gallon, funnel water heater.

- In one half of the lid of a 5-gallon honey or oil can, cut a hole and solder one piece of copper tubing that extends from 4 inches above the lid, down through the lid to the bottom of the can. Into the 4-inch length of tubing extending above the lid insert the end of a funnel that flares to 4½ inches in diameter. Solder the funnel to the tubing.
- In the other half of the lid, cut a hole and solder another piece of copper that extends from 8½ inches above the lid, down through the lid to 2½ inches below the lid.
- Curve the 8½ inches of tubing above the lid out and slightly over the edge of the can (fig. 26).
- Solder the two pieces of tubing together below the lid to make them sturdy.
- Fill the can with water up to the short copper tubing and let it heat over the fire or coals.
- When you desire hot water, pour cold water into the funnel and the hot water will come out of the curved tubing (fig. 27). The cold water will fall to the bottom of the can to be heated. The hot water will rise in the tube and will be expelled through the tubing. Place an empty can under the spout while the water is heating to catch the water as it heats and runs out of the tube (fig. 28).

Fig.26. Long copper tubing with funnel; short tubing with curved upper end

Fig.27. Cold water into funnel, hot water from curved copper tubing

34

Fig.28. Catching hot water as it heats and expands

Plastic-bag water heater. Let the sun heat water for you, with the help of a large, dark plastic garbage bag.

■ Pour about 4 gallons of water into a large, dark plastic bag.

■ Tie string or wire very tightly around the top of the bag.

■ Lay the bag on smooth ground in the sun (fig. 29). If you can't find a smooth spot, lay it on a poncho, a tarp stretched taut, or some other smooth surface so that sharp rocks or twigs will not puncture the bag. It is very important not to spread the tarp or place anything plastic over growing plants; it will kill them.

Depending upon the strength of the sun's rays, the water should become hot if the bag is left in the sun for the better part of a day. Then just undo the strings and pour water into a container.

Solar water heater. The water heater we have just described uses the sun as a heater. But its heat is not so concentrated as the one we will describe here.

Solar water heaters have long been used, and as early as the 1930s, southern California and Florida abounded in glass-covered heat collectors containing heating coils and a storage tank for hot water. Perhaps you have seen a solar water heater mounted atop a home.

The crude, makeshift designs of earlier days did a fair job of providing free hot water for domestic use, although standby heat sources were necessary for cloudy days or nighttime use. Today there are thousands of scientifically designed and highly efficient solar water

Fig.29. Plastic-bag water heater

heaters—particularly in Japan and Israel, where they compete successfully with gas and electric heaters.

A solar oven traps heat inside a glass-covered box, then transfers that heat to the food you want to cook. In a water heater the heat transfer is to water. The sun's rays warm water even without a special heating device. By adding a coil inside our hot box and circulating the water as it is warmed, we can make a more efficient water heater.

The heater described in this chapter is not intended for domestic use, but the 5-gallon tank would make a good supply for camping trips or for a cabin that has no provision for hot water. If desired, an enlarged version of the heater could be installed on a roof, connected to a water supply, and used as a permanent hot-water resource.

Materials:
1x4-inch wood—8 linear feet
½ inch plywood—two pieces 24x24 inches
Single-weight window glass—one piece, cut to measure
⅜-inch O.D. copper tubing—approximately 16 feet

Sheet metal—22x22 inches (copper or galvanized iron)
½-inch copper tubing—3 inches
½-inch valve—one
¾-inch hose fitting—one
5-gallon can—one
⅜-inch I.D. plastic tubing—10 feet
¼x1-½-inch wood screws—approximately thirty
Flat black paint—one pint
¼-inch stud and nut—one each
Carrying handle—one

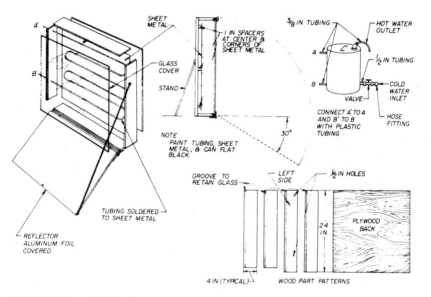

Fig.30. Solar water heater

Instructions:

- Begin the heater with the collector box itself. Make the sides of the box from 1-x-4 material. At the lumberyard have a groove cut ⅛ inch wide to a depth of ⅜ inch in the 1-x-4 board. Locate the cut ½ inch from one edge. This is the slot for the glass window.
- The next step is to cut the pieces to the proper length, being sure to keep the ends square both ways. The glass should fit snugly. Cut out a square of plywood 24 inches on a side and place the 1-x-4 pieces on it to make sure they fit.
- Assemble the side pieces to the back with wood screws.
- Take the box apart at this point and clean chips and shavings from

the holes. Drill two ½-inch holes in one of the side pieces, as shown in the drawing. These holes accommodate the copper tube coil, which will carry water from the tank to the collector and back again.

■ Now cement aluminum foil to the inside surface of the plywood base. This reflective material serves to bounce back radiated heat so that it will not be wasted.

■ Next, five small spacer blocks (1-inch cubes) are nailed into place, as shown in the drawing. Make these blocks the same thickness as the distance from the edge of the 1-x-4 piece to the ½-inch holes so that they hold the coil the proper distance from the plywood base. Small nails will be fine for attaching the spacers, but drill a hole through each block first to prevent splitting the wood.

■ With the box itself completed, you can begin work on the copper coil and the collector plate. These are important parts of the heater, since they transfer heat from the sun to the water inside the coil. Copper is a very good conductor and will quickly carry heat to the water. It is quite expensive, however, and you may want to substitute galvanized iron to cut the cost.

■ If you use a copper sheet, have it cut to the exact size. It is sold by weight, and there is no need to pay for scrap. Notice that the size specified allows ¼ inch of clearance all around the inside of the box. Before working with the copper sheet, trim a small piece from each corner at a 45-degree angle to prevent being cut by the sharp edges.

■ Bend the heating coil from ⅜-inch copper tube, the flexible kind that comes in a roll. The length called for in the list of materials allows for trimming. First straighten out the tubing, making it as flat and true as you can. It is quite soft, and a little time spent should result in a smooth job. Now lay the tube across the flat sheet of copper, with the proper length extending beyond the edge. Mark the start of the first bend in the tubing with a pencil and then carefully form it with your fingers into a U-shape. Work slowly and evenly so that you will not flatten the tube excessively.

After the first bend is made, replace the tubing on the sheet and make sure the bend is in the proper position and that sufficient tubing extends past the edge of the sheet. Mark the second bend and proceed as before. Continue to form the coil in this manner until the sheet is covered in a series of S-turns, as shown.

■ Trim the long end of the tubing; check the shape of the coil once more; then lay it on a flat surface to see that it is level. Spend as much time as is required to make the tubing lie perfectly flat, using your fingers and tapping lightly with a rubber or wooden mallet for the finishing touches. The tubing should touch the sheet along its full length for good heat transfer.

- When you are completely satisfied with the job, solder the copper coil to the sheet.
- Clean the tube and the sheet with emery cloth so that the solder will stick properly.
- Lay the sheet on a wooden surface (the inverted collector box itself will do nicely), and place the coil in position. Remember that the ends of the tubing must fit through the holes drilled in the 1x4.
- Now lay a board over the coil, and weight it to keep the tubing in place. You are ready for the soldering operation. If you have built the solar furnace, this would be a good time to try it out!

A small torch is handy for this purpose, and a soldering iron will do the job, too. If you aren't equipped for such work, have it done at a sheet-metal shop.

- Solder as shown on the drawing, about 6 inches apart. Be sure to hold the tubing flat to the sheet. Heat may cause the copper to warp slightly, but it will return to its flat position upon cooling.
- With the job completed, clean any excess soldering paste from the copper and paint the entire assembly flat black. Apply a second coat of paint for good measure, and set it aside until it is completely dry.
- The coil assembly may then be slipped into the box, with the ends of tubing carefully inserted into the ½-inch holes.
- Tack the copper sheet to the spacer blocks when you are sure it fits properly and will not have to be removed.
- Unscrew the top 1-x-4 piece. Slide a piece of cardboard into the grooves. Trim to fit, and have your glass supplier cut to this measure.
- Fit the glass into the slots, and replace the top piece.
- When you install the carrying handle, the collector is complete and you can begin work on the water tank.

A round, 5-gallon can with narrow, screw-top spout is used for the storage of heated water. The one in the photograph was a discarded oil can obtained from a local distributor. Other types are suitable and may be substituted if the round type shown is not available. For example, a square, lightweight can will fill the bill. This type is usually on sale at hardware and surplus stores.

- Clean the can of any residue of oil or other liquid. This is done for two reasons. First, we don't want the water contaminated, and second, heat from soldering operations might set fire to the liquid. So do the cleaning carefully and flush with water several times.

- Two short lengths of ⅜-inch copper tubing are soldered to the can. The location and dimensions are shown in the accompanying drawing. First drill a ¼-inch hole in each place a tube is to be installed. Next drive a center punch or other tapered piece of metal into the hole. This enlarges the hole and also forces the metal inward. Check frequently during this flaring process to insure a snug fit of tubing. The depression formed in this way will hold more solder and make a stronger point.

- If a painted can is used, it will be necessary to scrape the areas where soldering is to be done. When the metal is clean and bright, insert the tubing (which has been cleaned, too). Using a solar furnace, torch, or soldering iron, let solder flow into the depression and around the tube. This operation is easier if the can is positioned with the tube pointing straight up.

- The hot-water outlet is also a length of ⅜-inch tubing soldered to the screwed-on cap of the can. Use the "flaring" method again so that a strong joint will result. Notice that the tube is bent into a U-shape.

- You are now ready to do the plumbing for the cold-water supply line. Instead of ⅜-inch tubing, use ½-inch tubing for this connection. Attach a simple shutoff valve to the tube, using compression-type fittings that come with the valve. Your dealer will explain how these fittings are installed. Another short length of ½-inch tubing extends from the valve. The free end of this tubing is soldered inside a brass garden-hose fitting of the type used with a plastic hose.

- With the soldered joint made and the compression fittings tightened securely, you can connect the tank to the end of the garden hose and check for leaks. Turn on the water at the faucet; open the valve at the tank; and cork the tubes that will lead to the collector. When the tank is full, water will overflow from the hot-water supply outlet. Mark any leaks, drain the tank, and repair as necessary. The tank is now ready to be attached to the collector coil.

Your heater would be of little use if only the water in the coil itself became hot; this would be barely enough to wash one's hands. If you made a very large collector, the coils would hold ample hot water. Another method would be to install a pump to circulate water between coils and tank. This would cost more money and also make the heater more complicated. Fortunately, there is a phenomenon called *thermo-syphoning,* which will heat the whole tank of water. Thermosyphoning is the ability of water to circulate of its own accord when heated—given certain conditions. The most important of these conditions is that the supply tank be located *above* the coil.

The tank should be mounted on a stand, with the bottom of the tank about on a level with the top of the collector. As the coil heats water inside it, this water rises and is replaced by cooler water drawn from the bottom of the tank.

- Using the hinged prop, set up the collector facing the sun. Then place the tank on its stand to one side. Install the plastic hose between the two bottom tubes, using hose clamps for a watertight connection if necessary. Attach one end of the second plastic hose to the upper tube of the collector, but leave the other end free.
- Fill the tank. When water flows from the open plastic hose, block the hose with your finger until water also flows from the top circulation tube of the tank. Then quickly slide the hose onto the tube and clamp it. This prevents air bubbles from being trapped in the lines. When the hot-water outlet overflows, close the tank valve.

Operation of the heater is simple. You will notice that the upper hose quickly gets hot, while the lower one stays relatively cool. Water is circulating now, and eventually, all of it will be warmed by the coils.

- To draw hot water, open the valve at the bottom of the tank. Cold water comes in and forces hot water out of the top (fig. 31).
- To increase the heating capacity of your water heater, add a reflector panel that will also serve as a protective cover for the glass when you

Fig.31. Water tank

store the heater. One reflector, set at 30 degrees, will add 50 percent more heat. You can add four, if desired, and greatly increase the heating capacity. The water heater in the photograph uses one reflector, hinged at the bottom and secured at the top. A hole in the reflector fits over the ¼-inch stud and is held in place with a nut when the heater is stored or being carried about.

- Make the reflector(s) of ½-inch plywood, faced with aluminized Mylar, aluminum foil, or similar reflecting material. Attach to the heater with hinges, allowing one reflector to fold down on top of the other as shown in the drawing. Lengths of cord hold the reflector panels at the proper angle. As with the oven, when the reflector is closed, it protects the glass cover of the heater.

You can use the heater in a more portable version—on a camping trip, for instance, where there is no water-pressure supply available.

- Simply close the inlet valve, fill the tank through the top, and let the water heat.
- To draw hot water, tip the tank and pour out water through the spout. Replace as needed.

Kitchen Equipment

Container for liquid oil. A soap container with a pop-up top is useful for storing and using liquid oil (fig. 32).

- Fill the clean soap container with liquid oil (salad or cooking oil).
- Pop the top down until you are ready to use the oil.

Frisbee plate nester. On picnic and car trips, campers often use paper plates. The inexpensive kind does not hold its shape well unless it is reinforced by an additional plate or a "nester." A Frisbee, often taken along on camping trips for fun, is just the right shape to fit under a paper plate to help it hold its shape (fig. 33). It may pay to invest in a few more Frisbees!

Fire-Starter

- Roll newspapers tightly to 4 inches in diameter.
- Tape around the outsides to hold the paper together. Cut it in 1-inch sections with a band saw or sharp knife.

Fig.32. Liquid oil container

Fig.33. Frisbee as a nest for a paper plate

Fig.34. Strip of newspaper for tinder

Fig.35. Newspaper-wax fire

- Place rolls of paper in melted wax, letting the paper absorb as much wax as possible; remove and place on paper to cool.

    (Candle wax from your local hobby store is usually the least expensive kind.)

- When the sections are ready to use, merely pull out about ten inches of the center and use it for a fire starter (fig. 34). In snow or at times when tinder is not available, uncoil the center of the paper, light it, and let the whole roll burn (fig. 35).

    Small pieces of newspaper can also be rolled into smaller rolls, tied with string, and dipped in wax. Caution: When melting wax, use a double boiler so that the wax will not ignite because of its low combustion point.

43

Fuel (rolled logs). Take several sections of paper tightly rolled and tie with wire (figs. 36 to 38). These can later be used as logs in the fireplace or on a camping trip.

Fig.36. Overlapped paper for rolled log   Fig.37. Rolling newspaper log

Fig.38. Tying newspaper log with wire

44

SHELTER AND SLEEPING BAGS

Since the beginning of time, man has sought to protect himself from wind, rain, snow, sun, insects, and animals by the use of shelter. Primitive man sought shelter in caves, overhanging rocks, lean-tos, and teepees. Today, the selection and types of camping shelters are limitless. They range from tarps or sheets of plastic to multicompartmental tents. This chapter will concern itself with the characteristics of good shelter, tent accessories, selecting a site for shelter, pitching and staking a tent, care of shelter, and the kinds of sleeping bags to use on a car-camping trip.

CHARACTERISTICS OF GOOD SHELTER

Sufficient Capacity

How many people will be expecting to be sheltered at your camp? One, three, six? How many little ones, big ones? How much equipment will have to be stored, along with all the bodies, in case of rain? Remember that 17 square feet of space per person is required for comfortable sleeping, 25 square feet per person for general living.

If the tents are to be transported by car, you can afford to take ones that are large and comfortable, with ample room for several people to stand up. If you choose any of the following styles, you should be assured of plenty of room for family living: umbrella (fig. 39), cabin (fig. 40), Springbar® (fig. 41), and modular or multicompartmental (fig. 42).

Weight and Bulk

Tents used in car camping can be heavier and bulkier than lightweight tents because it is not necessary to conserve weight or space. Tent and poles may weigh up to 40 pounds and more.

Fig.39. Umbrella tent. Better headroom than teepee tent, but sloping walls limit efficient use of floor space.

Fig.40. Cabin tent (wall tent). Basic "A" structure plus vertical walls. One disadvantage: guy ropes require time and effort to set up.

46

Fig.41. Springbar® tent. Requires no guy ropes; provides good headroom and useable space. Easy to erect and dismantle.

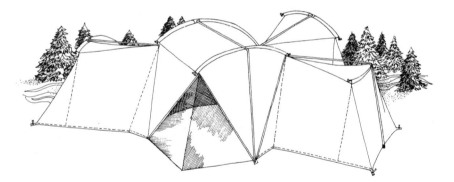

Fig.42. Modular (multicompartmental) tent. Different components combine into various tenting and shelter arrangements: kitchens, bedrooms, living rooms.

Ease of Assembly

Setting up a large tent often requires two or more people working together. Even though the tent is big, with several poles for support of the tent, most modern tent designs make the task of assembling remarkably simple.

Materials and Construction

Cotton or cotton duck is commonly used in larger, family-sized tents. Cotton "breathes" better than nylon, but is heavier and bulkier. It expands to fill the pores of the material when it rains and makes the tent water-repellent. Its heaviness makes a good shelter in the wind. Because the price of cotton fluctuates from year to year, some tent manufacturers try using synthetic materials to offset the price, but they are taking a risk. The roof and sidewalls of a tent, at the very least, should be of cotton to make the tent livable.

In choosing tent fabric, consider the weight as well as the quality. The weight is designated by the number of ounces in one square yard of material. Generally speaking, the highest-quality material on the current market weighs 10 ounces per square yard. For a large tent, 5 or 6 ounces is a marginal weight. (Quite often lightweight material will contain fillers for water repellency.)

The quality is determined by the density, or thread count. The greater the density, the higher the quality. Good material and good workmanship generally go together.

The stress points of a tent should be reinforced with a double seam, and the seams should run in the direction of the support, usually vertically, not horizontally.

If you are looking for good construction, you can usually find it with a well-established manufacturer who, year by year, makes improvements on his tents.

TENT ACCESSORIES

To be caught without necessary equipment when you are attempting to erect a tent is a sure-fire guarantee of a frustrating experience. Give a little forethought to those helps.

Stakes

Don't rely on the pegs you buy with your tent to be sufficient for all your pitching needs. Aluminum wire skewers work well in most places, but if the ground is very rocky, you might need metal skewers. If you find yourself in a sandy spot, strong plastic stakes with I-beams will

48

hold well. A cement nail will hold in some solid rocks. If the ground is too soft to stake, guy lines can be tied to logs or rocks which are called dead men (fig. 43). They can also be buried in the ground for more solid security.

Fig.43. Ways of making a dead man

Poles

If you have room, take along extra poles in case a high wind or a clumsy hand breaks one. Of course, if you are careful to choose strong poles, you won't have this trouble.

Guy Lines

Some tents must be rigged with guy lines for extra support and for stabilizing the tent. Most tents today do not require guy lines except during a heavy wind.

Shock Cord

If you do use guy lines when the wind is blowing, a shock cord is helpful in keeping the line from snapping. Simply tie a short length of sturdy rubber to the guy line, about midway in its length. Make a half loop in the guy line and tie the other end of the rubber piece to the guy line just below the loop. As the wind blows, the rubber stretches, relieving tension that ordinarily would be on the guy line (fig. 44).

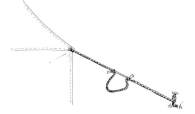

Fig.44. Shock cord on guy line

49

SELECTING A SITE

Several factors must be considered (if you have a choice these days) in choosing a site for your shelter.

Protection from Wind

Wind tearing at the flaps of your shelter can create a miserable experience for you.

Whenever possible, find a campsite away from the prevailing direction of the wind. Wind will not only intensify the cold, it can make your tent a noisy, flapping place as well, making it difficult for you to sleep.

Protection from Insects

One of the most tormenting experiences of a camper is to be attacked by insects. Your shelter should be as nearly airtight as possible (insect-proof-size holes in netting, for one thing), but, also, try the following suggestions to help you escape such a situation.

Avoid damp areas. Insects breed in moist habitats. The drier your campsite, the freer from insects you will be.

Search for a breeze. Insects don't like breezes. If you can find a site with a constant movement of air, your chances of avoiding an insect onslaught are better.

Protection from Bears

If you are in bear country, don't take any chances. And don't believe anyone who assures you "the bears around here are tame." Too many tragedies have occurred for you to believe such nonsense.

Put food out of reach. Store food outside the tent, and have it high enough that a bear cannot reach it and far enough away from camp that the bear won't associate it with your camp.

Eat outside. If possible, refrain from eating in your tent, where the odor of food will linger and invite a bear's exploration. Food odor also clings to clothing; try to keep it clean. If you are a woman, don't use perfume, and keep clean during your menstrual cycle.

Do not feed bears. Once fed, a bear will come searching for more food. If you are asleep and unable to grant his desires, he may become dangerous.

Protection from Cold

If you dress in lightweight layers, you will sleep more warmly than in one heavy piece of clothing (although too many layers will not allow your body to warm the bag). Add padding between you and the ground, and take care to pitch your tent where it will receive the morning sun that will warm the inside of your shelter.

Protection from Fire

Common sense will probably tell you to avoid burning dry pine boughs or weeds that will shoot sparks toward your tent. Be careful when building a fire on a windy day. Pitch your tent so that the wind cannot blow fire and sparks in its direction.

PITCHING AND STAKING

If you can learn to pitch your tent successfully, at least half the battle of trying to enjoy the out-of-doors will be won. The following suggestions might be of help.

Contour of Ground

Select a spot as level as possible and remove rocks and twigs (but remember to replace them when you leave). If no level spot is available, you'll want your head to be uphill.

It is no longer in good taste to dig a trench around your tent. Join the cause of the environmentalists and refrain from doing this. If possible, pitch your tent on high ground so that water runs away from it instead of into it.

Rehearse Pitching Your Tent

If your tent is new and you are unfamiliar with the steps required to pitch it, have a dress rehearsal. First, stake the corners securely, stretching the floor out full length so that it is smooth and flat, not loose and wrinkled. With the instructions at your elbow, follow the procedures step by step, setting up your tent in your back yard or in a park near you. Sprinkle water on the tent to see if it leaks. Disassemble it and do it over again, if necessary. Your confidence will strengthen with your increasing expertise.

CARE OF SHELTER

When you have decided upon the type of shelter best for you and have spent your hard-earned cash for it, you will expect it to serve you well. Remember that if you treat it well, it will reciprocate.

Keep It Dry

Although nylon will not mildew as easily as cotton if it remains wet, the zipper tapes will actually rot. Tents that are all or partly cotton will mildew. While you are breaking camp, let the sun dry your tent thoroughly. Even without the sun, it will dry if you give it time. If you can't take the time, roll it up and stow it, but unfold it and dry it out either at home or at your next camping spot before it has time to mildew. Then store it in a dry place—probably not in your basement. Cotton and cotton-wrapped nylon thread will mildew and rot even on a nylon tent. When storing, hang your tent instead of laying it down where water and mice can ruin it.

Protect It from Puncture

We have mentioned that before you pitch your tent, you should remove rocks and twigs from the area where you will set it up. Be careful when you pitch the tent under a tree because of falling branches. After it is pitched, keep rocks and sharp objects outside the tent. If you track them in, get rid of them immediately. Punctures will turn into rips, and soon you will need a new tent.

When you pack your tent, cover the stake or skewer points with canvas so they will not poke holes in the tent.

Keep It Clean

Although the outside of a tent should never be washed (so that it won't begin to leak), the inside should be kept free from things like gummy pitch and particles of food. Imagine the mess and the odor if you should leave sticky, greasy food in a folded tent for a time.

Two things can help keep the floor of your shelter clean: (1) The material should be nylon or polyester with a vinyl coating to resist acids in soil and to make it easy to mop. (A patch of vinyl can be attached if a hole appears.) (2) A whiskbroom can keep the dirt brushed out. You'll find the little extra time it takes will be well worth it.

This is only a quick overview of the principles involved in choosing and using outdoor shelters. Start with these basics to find out the best kind for you. And happy tenting to you.

SLEEPING BAGS

In car camping, as well as in all outdoor activities, a good night's sleep is imperative for the enjoyment of the next day's events. The types of sleeping bags vary from a blanket used in the hot desert to a down-filled bag or fiber-filled bag used in the cold. Discussed in this chapter are the heavier synthetic-filled bags which are best transported by automobiles. Later, in chapter 8, bags to be used in lightweight camping are described.

Cuts of Bags

The rectangular bag is just that—a bag the same size at the bottom as at the top. The zipper on this bag zips across the bottom and up the side, allowing the bag to be opened out. Thus, it can be used as a quilt at times, or it can be zipped to another bag to be used as a double bag. Another advantage of the rectangular bag is that it has space for moving about, providing greater comfort.

One disadvantage of the rectangular bag is that its greater space requires more body energy to warm it on cold nights. But it remains a popular bag for car campers because it is comfortable, it is the shape of a bed, and weight is not an important factor.

The modified rectangular bag is similar to the rectangular except that it tapers in toward the bottom, cutting down on the weight and the space required to transport it. It restricts movement in the feet area a little more than does the rectangular bag.

Materials Used

Covers for sleeping bags range from light canvas tops with flannel lining to synthetic materials for both top and lining. Most car bags are filled with synthetic fibers, which are polyester, Dacron 88, Dacron Fiberfill II®, and Polar Guard®. The price for these synthetics varies with the performance of the bag and with the type of fill.

Polyester. The least expensive fill for a bag is polyester. A blend of different polyester filaments of low efficiency, it is inexpensive but fills the needs of those on limited budgets. This is not recommended for cold-weather bags.

Dacron 88. A medium-priced filling is Dacron 88, a dense, heavy fiber. It comes in mat form with some quilting evident. It usually requires dry cleaning. It is more effective than polyesters but not as efficient as Dacron Fiberfill II® and Polar Guard®.

Dacron Fiberfill II® and Polar Guard®. Dacron Fiberfill II® and Polar Guard® is hollow, short-stapled fiber. The fibers are highly mobile and require quilting to contain them. Better-grade bags should have multiple layers for greater efficiency.

Polar Guard® is an "endless" fiber which requires little in the way of baffles or quilts. It is very efficient.

Neither fiber absorbs water, so when wet they will dry quickly and are almost always machine-washable. They do not need to be rolled but can be stuffed into a sack when storing or carrying.

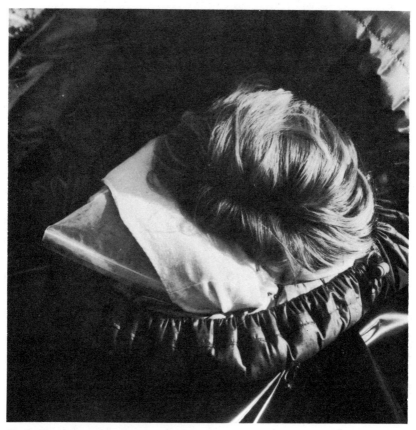

Fig.45. Zip-Lock bag used as a pillow

Less expensive than any of the above is a bedroll made out of blankets, as described in *Roughing It Easy.* The most expensive fill is goose or duck down, discussed in chapter eight of this book.

Don't wait to go camping until you can buy a fancy bag. If you can have a comfortable, warm night's rest with blankets, then you have accomplished two goals—(1) you've had a fun camping trip and (2) you've been able to save your money.

Sleeping-Out Suggestions

■ A quick pillow can be made by blowing up a large Zip-Lock bag to the desired size and placing a shirt or slipcover over it (fig. 45).

- Another pillow can be made by folding your parka, placing it in a case, and using it for a pillow. When your head is cold and you do not have a head section to your sleeping bag, place your head up into the sleeve area of your parka and use it as a cap. Or you can wear a stocking cap to bed.
- When your feet become cold, there are several things you can do to help retain the heat:

    1. Wear wool socks to bed.

    2. Early in the evening, place a rock beside the fire (fig. 46) and let the heat slowly penetrate into it. Be sure the rock doesn't contain moisture. Get it from a dry area. A rock with moisture can explode. Wrap it with foil and place it at the foot of your sleeping bag. Caution: Make sure you can comfortably handle the rock before placing it in the bottom of your bag. This will prevent any unexpected burn holes. If the rock is a little warmer than anticipated, it can be rolled in newspapers so that it isn't quite so hot. Never put an extremely hot rock into the bottom of your bag. Be especially careful with hot rocks in synthetic bags. The bags melt at comparatively low temperatures.

    3. Put your feet into the sleeve of a parka or sweater.

    4. Take a hot-water bottle to bed with you.

Fig.46. Rock heating by fire

Fig.47. Newspaper under bag

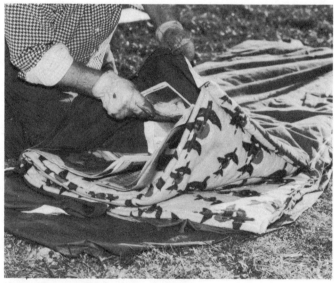

Fig.48. Newspaper in top lining of bag

- Further insulation: When you are cold, you can insulate your bag by placing newspapers or cardboard under it. Newspapers can also be placed over your bag, preferably under a slip cover to keep the papers in place (figs. 47 and 48).

Fig.49. Clamped pie tin on rocks over coals

Fig.50. Coals placed on lid of pie tin

58

ENCLOSED AND CONCENTRATED HEAT

An oven can be created by enclosing heat and letting the air circulate. Some materials used to enclose heat are foil, cans, a cardboard box lined with foil, and a Dutch oven. The reflector oven is an exception to this. Food is placed on the reflector oven rack and placed close enough to the flames so that the concentrated heat cooks the food.

Pie-Tin Oven

Two pie tins can be used to make an oven that will bake biscuits, pie, cake, pizza, and other foods.

- Oil one pie tin and place food in it.
- Turn a second pie tin upside down over the first tin to make a lid.
- Use three or four metal clamps (the kind used to clamp paper together) an equal distance apart on the lip of the pans.
- Place three rocks or spikes in a bed of coals high enough to elevate the pie-tin oven 1 inch above the coals (fig. 49).
- Place coals on lid (fig. 50). If many coals are desired, a foil collar can be made by folding a length of foil two or three times and hooking it together at the ends so that the collar will fit around the pie tin to hold the coals.

The item to be cooked should be done in about the same length of time as it would be in a home oven.

Either pliers or asbestos gloves will be needed to remove the clamps. Care should be taken to brush the coals off before opening the lid.

Chicken Under Inverted Can

The following cooking method is a basic oven. Many foods can be cooked this way.

- Sharpen one end of a sweet bark stick 14 to 20 inches long and thrust it into the ground to make a hole which will be used later (fig. 51).

- Remove the stick, split the other end of it, and wedge a clean stone between the split ends to hold them apart approximately 2 or 3 inches.
- Sharpen both split ends.
- Insert the split end of the stick through its opening and into its rib cage so that it will not slip down on the stick while it is cooking (fig. 52).
- Place a piece of foil over the previously made hole; push the end of the stick through the foil (fig. 53).
- Push the end of the stick into the ground so that a 5-gallon honey can (with one end cut out) can be set down over the chicken until the can rests on the ground (fig. 54). The chicken should not touch the sides of the can or it will burn.
- Place hot coals or charcoal briquets on top of, around the bottom and stacked up the sides of the can (fig. 55).

Hardwood coals are needed to keep the temperature up. The cooking time will vary from 90 to 120 minutes, depending on how brown you want the chicken.

So that you will not "pepper" the chicken with ashes when you remove the can, brush off the coals from the top first.

Fig.51. Hole formed for stick

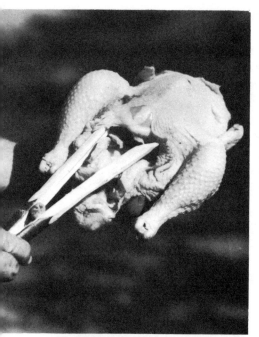
Fig.52. Pronged stick inserted into chicken

Fig.53. Stick through foil and into hole

Fig.54. Chicken covered with five-gallon can

Fig.55. Can covered with hot coals

61

Inverted Dutch Oven and Frying Pan

Fried foods can be cooked on the inverted lid of a Dutch oven at the same time that a delicious pie is cooking for lunch or dinner.

To master this simple time-saving method, dig a small hole about 9 to 12 inches in diameter by 3 to 4 inches deep. Place coals about ¾" high in the hole and place the rack on the ground. The rack should be 2 to 3 inches above the coals (fig. 56). Place pie on the rack (or other food to be cooked in pan), turn 12-inch Dutch oven with legs upside down over it (fig. 57). Dutch oven should not touch sides of pan. Spread coals over the bottom of the Dutch oven. Place the Dutch oven lid upside down on the legs of the oven so that you will have a surface to cook on. Let the lid warm for a few minutes, then place the food to be fried on the lid (fig. 58). The pie should take approximately the same amount of time as it does in your oven at home. Steak, eggs, bacon, hamburger, or anything that fries may be cooked on the lid (fig. 59).

Inverted Lid Oven

An oven can be constructed by using a large lid from a roasting pan or large container. A rack with legs, such as a backpacker's rack or a large wire grill, is placed above the coals. Make a small pan by using foil 2 inches smaller than the circumference of the lid. Place the lid over the foil and let the hot air circulate around the edges to bake the food. To regulate the heat, raise and lower the rack.

An aluminum dishpan with an empty thread spool bolted to it as a handle may also be used as an oven (fig. 60). To attach the spool to the pan, make a big hole large enough for a ⅛-inch bolt 3 inches long in the center of the pan. Use two washers, one on top of the spool and one inside next to the lid, before tightening the nut.

Muffin-Tin Oven

Two muffin tins make a very serviceable outdoor oven.
- Line compartments of muffin tin with cupcake liners. If liners are not available, oil the compartments.
- Fill the compartments with different foods, including hamburger, vegetables, and muffin dough or cake batter (fig. 61).

62

Fig.56. Rack over coals

Fig.57. Pie to be baked
under Dutch oven

Fig.58. Pie baking and food frying

Fig.59. Baked pie and fried food

Fig.60. Inverted lid oven

Fig.61. Muffin tin filled with food

- Season the foods.
- For easy cleaning of top pan, place a liner over the foods that might stick (fig. 62).
- Fit the second muffin tin over the first.
- Clamp the muffin tins together with four large clamps, the kind used to clamp paper together.
- Keeping the muffin tins level, place them on four rocks over medium-hot coals and put hot coals on top of the "oven," making sure that more coals cover the meat end than the dough end (fig. 63).
- Cook for 25 to 35 minutes.

Fig.62 Muffin tin liners to keep food from sticking	Fig.63. Clamped muffin tin with coals covering top

Hot Box or Fireless Cooker

Want another way of cooking a meal while you're out hiking or fishing? Try this one.

- Bring a one-pot meal to a boil in your Dutch oven. Let it cook about half the recommended cooking time.
- Take it from the fire and place it in a large cardboard or wooden box or a ground box (a hole in the ground shaped like a box).
- Insert 2 to 3 inches of newspaper on all sides of the box as snugly as possible to prevent heat loss. The newspapers can be placed in the box beforehand (fig. 64).

The food will continue to cook and will stay hot for hours. The time depends on how good the insulation is. Other types of kettles will work but not as well as heavy, heat-retaining metals such as cast iron and heavy aluminum.

64

Fig.64. Cooked food in hot box

Cardboard Box/Foil Oven

The efficiency of this little oven-in-the-wilds will delight you (fig. 65). I baked a cake in it, among other things, and it was as good as if I had baked it in my oven at home. The oven is fun to make, too, before you start out on your camping trip.

- Cut the top off a cardboard box that is approximately 1 foot square. (The box should be about 1 inch larger all the way around than the baking pan that will be used inside it.) With the top cut off, the box should be laid on its side. The cut-off portion of the box will be the opening to the oven.
- Line the entire inside of the box with foil—the shiny side out.
- Close all seams on the outside of the box with duct tape (heat-resistant tape) to keep heat from leaking out.
- On both sides of the box, near the bottom, punch two holes about ¼ inch in diameter for ventilation. If the coals do not continue to burn, you may have to punch more holes.

- At the back, high in one corner, punch two small holes quite close together. Insert a twisty (from a plastic bag) through one hole. Put the other end through the hole inside the box and place the thermometer through the loop made by the twisty. Pull the twisty, and twist the ends together.

  For the door of the oven, cut a piece of cardboard about ¼ inch larger than the hole to the oven. Line the inside of the door with foil. On the outside of the door, tape a handle shaped from cardboard.
- If you want a window in the oven door, cut a square hole in the door and cover it with see-through oven wrap, secured by the duct tape.
- Secure with the duct tape the top of the door to the top of the opening so that the door swings free, as if it were hinged.
- To make the rack inside the oven, use a piece of rack (nonclimbable wire or similar racks will work. Check with your local hardware store; they should be able to help you) about 20 inches long and 6 inches wide. Bend both ends of the rack at right angles about 4½ inches and stand the rack inside the oven.
- For insulation, pour pebbles or dirt into a pan that will fit into the bottom of the oven. (Foil can be placed across the dirt or sand in order to elevate the briquets a little bit so that more oxygen can get to the briquets.) Place fifteen to twenty hot briquets on top of the pebbles.

Fig.65. Cardboard box oven

Fig.66. Cake in cardboard box oven

Fig.67. Cardboard box oven baking

When you are ready to use the oven, preheat it to desired heat. When the food to be baked is placed on the rack (fig. 66), the temperature will go down temporarily but should rise again as the food cooks. Place a rock against the outside of the oven door to keep it closed (fig. 67). A small gap is okay, but large spaces will let the heat out.

The briquets will hold their heat for about one hour. If you expect to use the oven for a longer period of time, add briquets gradually while the first ones are still hot.

Methods from *Roughing It Easy*

In *Roughing It Easy* these methods are described in detail, but we will show here seven ways from that book that heat circulates according to these principles (figs. 68 to 74). Arrows show the way heat circulates.

Fig.68. Enclosed heat circulating inside Dutch oven

Fig.69. Enclosed heat circulating inside tin-can stove oven

**Fig.70.
Enclosed heat circulating inside can-inside-can oven**

Fig.72. Enclosed heat circulating in loaf-tin-in-can oven

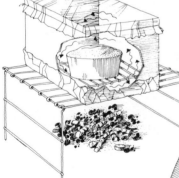

**Fig.71.
Enclosed heat circulating in cardboard-box oven**

Fig.73. Concentrated heat in reflector oven

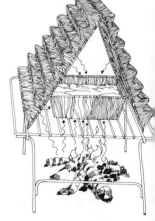

Fig.74. Concentrated heat in foil-pan oven

RECIPES FOR ENCLOSED AND CONCENTRATED HEAT

Hot meals—breakfasts, lunches, dinners, from appetizers to desserts—you can cook them all in the wilderness. Here are some recipes for you to begin with, using the enclosed or concentrated (oven) method. Try your own favorites, too!

Dump Cake

Method: Dutch oven
Time: 45 minutes to 1 hour
(For easy cleaning, line Dutch oven with foil.)

- Place in Dutch oven — 1 size 2½ can sliced peaches with juice
- Dump over top of peaches and spread evenly — 1 white or yellow cake mix (fig. 75)
- Stir enough to moisten cake mix
- Dot top with — ¼ pound butter or margarine

Place coals on top and bottom of Dutch oven and bake for 45 minutes.

Variations: Fruits such as pineapple, cherries, apples, and others may be substituted for the peaches. Nuts can also be sprinkled over the top. The flavor of the cake may also be varied.

Fig.75. Dump cake

Gourmet German Pancakes

Method: 12-inch Dutch oven (with three ¾-inch rocks in bottom) and one pie pan (fig. 76).

Time: 15 minutes

- In pie tin placed on rocks in bottom of Dutch oven, melt   1 tablespoon butter
- Pour into pie tin ¼-inch deep batter (fig. 77) made by mixing

3 eggs
½ cup flour
½ cup milk
salt

Put lid on and place on bed of coals, with several coals on top of the lid. (The Dutch oven must be very hot, equal to a 400°F. oven.)

Cook for 10 to 15 minutes, then remove lid. The pancake batter will have risen up the sides and browned (fig. 78). Divide into the number of portions to be served and place a mixture of drained raspberries, sliced bananas, and chunk pineapple (or other types of fruit) on the pancake, sprinkle with brown sugar, and dot with sour cream.

Deep-Pan Pizza

Method: Pie pan oven

Time: 20 minutes

- Fry in saucepan or Dutch oven   ½ pound hamburger
- Oil   one pie pan
- Cover other pie pan and its sides with   1 or 2 flour tortillas (fig. 79)
- Add cooked meat
- Pour to ⅓ inch deep into tortillas   thick spaghetti sauce
- Dice and add to the spaghetti sauce and meat   ½ green pepper and ½ onion
- Slice or grate and cover all of the above with   ½ pound mozzarella cheese (fig. 80)

Turn the oiled pie pan lid upside down and clamp to bottom pie pan. Place on rocks above coals and put hot coals on top. Cook until

Fig.76. Rocks in Dutch oven and butter in pan

Fig.77. Batter in pie pan

Fig.78. Cooked German pancake

Fig.79. Flour tortilla in pie tin   **Fig.80. Covering deep-pan pizza with cheese**

green pepper and onions are softened. Cut pizza with a knife and remove with a spatula.

Variation: Substitute any of your favorite pizza ingredients for any of the above.

Dutch Oven Roast Beef

Method: Dutch oven
Time: 4-6 hours

■ Braise	1 pot roast
■ Add	1 can consommé (10½ ounces)
■ Plus	(vegetable amounts vary with number of people)
	carrots
	potatoes
	onions
	salt and pepper
	½ package dried onion soup

Place lid on Dutch oven leaving a space between the meat and the lid. Place the Dutch oven in the fire pit, cover it with coals, which has been lined with dry rocks (rocks with moisture will explode) and had a glowing fire in for about 1-1½ hours. Depending on size of roast it should be cooked in 4 to 6 hours. Gravy could be made from juices by thickening with flour (add flour to cold water and make a smooth paste before adding it to boiling juices).

Fig.81. Wacky cake

Wacky Cake

Method: Dutch oven
Time: 30 to 45 minutes

- Mix into a plastic Zip-Lock bag

Dry ingredients:
3 cups flour
2 teaspoons soda
2 cups sugar
1 teaspoon salt
6 tablespoons cocoa

- In a pint jar or container, mix

Liquid ingredients:
2 tablespoons vinegar
2 teaspoons vanilla
¾ cup oil

If your plastic bag is a heavy one, you can add the liquid ingredients to it and hand mix by squeezing. If not, combine the dry ingredients in a cake pan and mix well. Combine the liquids in a pint jar. Make three wells in the dry mixture and add the liquids. Blend with a spoon until moist. Bake in a foil-lined Dutch oven for 30 to 45 minutes. When the cake is done, remove it from the oven and sprinkle it immediately with 1 to 2 cups miniature marshmallows and ½ to 1 cup milk chocolate chips (fig. 81). Place lid on oven and let sit for five minutes or until ready to serve. The chocolate chips and marshmallows will melt and glaze the top of the cake. Package cake mixes can also be used.

Dutch Oven Enchilada Casserole

Method: Dutch oven or kettle
Time: 15 minutes for frying; 15 for baking

■ Brown together	2 pounds ground beef
	1 teaspoon salt
	1 large onion, chopped
■ Add and simmer together	1 can tomato soup
	(10¾-ounce can)
	2 cans enchilada mild sauce
	(10 ounces)
	1 can water (10 ounces)
■ Remove ¾ of meat mixture from pan. Place over top of remaining mixture	3 corn tortillas uncooked
■ Add a layer of meat mixture. Place over the top	¼ pound grated or sliced cheese
■ Add a layer of meat mixture	
■ Place over the top	3 corn tortillas
■ Add another layer of meat mixture	
■ Place over the top	¼ pound grated or sliced cheese

Place lid over pan and let simmer. Serves six generous portions.

Chicken Supreme

Method: Dutch oven
Time: 1½ to 2 hours

- Cut into pieces   1 chicken
- Roll chicken pieces in   flour
- Sprinkle floured chicken with   salt, garlic salt, and meat
                                                     tenderizer (optional)
- Brown chicken in Dutch oven in   1 to 2 cups hot oil (fig. 82)
- Pour oil out of Dutch oven into a
  can, and over browned chicken in
  Dutch oven pour   1 can tomato juice (32 ounces)
                                                     1 can drained mushrooms

Cover and place coals on lid and let simmer at low heat for approximately 1 hour or until chicken is tender.

Fig.82. Chicken browning in Dutch oven

75

Rice Pudding

Method: Dutch oven
Time: 30 minutes

- Mix together

2 cups cooked rice
4 cups milk
½ cup brown sugar
½ teaspoon cinnamon
½ cup raisins
2 eggs, beaten
pinch of salt
1 teaspoon vanilla

Pour into greased Dutch oven. Leave about 1 inch of air space under the Dutch oven lid so that the milk does not scorch. Cover with lid. Place coals on top and around bottom of Dutch oven and bake.

Baked Eggs

Method: Muffin tin
Time: About 10 to 15 minutes

- Into the greased cups of one
  muffin tin, break
- Add to each egg

number of eggs desired
1 tablespoon milk
grated cheese
salt and pepper
½ slice cooked bacon

Put another muffin tin over and clamp. Place over low-heat coals, and place coals on lid to bake. Use cupcake liners for cleaning ease.

Muffin-Tin Dinner for Two

Method: Muffin tin
Time: 25 to 30 minutes

- Cover the inside of two
  8-compartment muffin tins with   oil or grease
- In two compartments of each tin
  (top and bottom), pack tightly   a meatloaf mixture
- Cut and place in two

compartments of bottom muffin tin	carrots
■ Cut up and place in the next two compartments of bottom tin	potatoes (salted)
■ Fill last two compartments of bottom tin nearly level with	muffin dough or cake dough
■ Season carrots with	a little salt, brown sugar, and pineapple (if desired)
■ To meatloaf mixture, add	salt and catsup

When all compartments are filled, fit one muffin tin over the other, matching meatloaf to meatloaf. Clamp the muffin tins together with four large clamps, the kind used to clamp paper together.

Keeping the "oven" level, place it on medium-hot coals, and place hot coals on top of it, making sure that more coals cover the meat end than the dough end.

(Aluminum foil may be used to line the muffin tin compartments for easier cleaning, or you may use cupcake liners.)

Meat Pie

Method: Dutch oven
Time: 3 to 3½ hours

■ Cook until done	beef or chicken (salted and peppered)
■ Cut up the tender meat into the broth it was cooked in	
■ Add to the meat and broth	potatoes carrots onions a little milk (if desired)
■ Cook until vegetables are done	
■ Make small biscuits from	3 cups flour 4 teaspoons baking powder 1 teaspoon salt 3 tablespoons shortening (or bacon fat 1⅓ cups milk or water

Cover meat and vegetables with biscuits and cook until the dough is done and the tops are brown.

Cheesy Snackeroos

Method: Dutch oven
Time: Approximately 25 minutes

- Prepare according to package instructions

  1 package corn bread or corn muffin mix (8½ ounces)

- Add to this mixture

  ⅓ cup grated Parmesan cheese

- Place in well-greased Dutch oven
- Sprinkle over the top

  ¾ cup chopped salted peanuts
  ⅓ cup grated Parmesan cheese
  ½ teaspoon garlic salt

- Melt in a separate pan and drizzle over the top

  ¼ cup melted margarine

Cover Dutch oven and bake over coals 25 minutes or until light brown. Cool slightly before cutting in wedges and serving.

FREE HEAT

As with your broiler at home that produces dry heat, food can be placed above coals on a stick, a spit, or a rack to create the same cooking condition. Care needs to be taken to rotate the food at the right time. Food held at a distance will cook more slowly, and the heat will penetrate more. Larger items such as chicken should be kept at a distance; the heat will penetrate and cook the food all the way through.

Vertical Spit

Chicken and other items may be cooked with this method, which is like an uncovered oven.

- Drive four 3-foot-long metal stakes into the ground 12 to 14 inches apart, forming a square.
- Cut four pieces of 1-inch mesh chicken wire 2 feet long and 9 holes wide (leave 9 holes and cut tenth in half).
- Fasten the two long sides of each roll together, making long, tube-like wire cages.
- Slip each wire cage vertically down over each metal stake and fill each wire cage with briquets (one row of briquets from ground to top of cage) (fig. 83).
- Light the briquets. After they are hot, wrap aluminum foil around the outside of the four stakes to hold the heat in the enclosed area (fig. 84).
- Make a tripod out of three sticks or lengths of metal about 4 feet long, tying them together at the top with rope.
- Place the tripod over the four stakes so that the top of the tripod is centered over them.
- Tie the wings and legs of a chicken (fryer) to its body.
- Tie a length of heavy string to the legs of the chicken long enough so that when the other end of the string is tied to the top of the tripod, the chicken will dangle about 3 to 4 inches above the ground (fig. 85).

It will take about an hour to an hour and a half to roast the chicken. When you baste the chicken with barbecue sauce, do it the last 15 minutes, or the sauce will burn.

Fig.83. Briquets in wire cages

Fig.84. Wrapping foil around vertical barbeque

Fig.85. Tripod centered over stakes suspending chicken

Plank or Split-Log

Fish, steak, or any meat about ½ to 1 inch thick can be cooked this way. Steak or thick pieces of meat will have to be removed and turned to finish cooking (fig. 86).

- Use a clean board or split a piece of firewood at least 6 inches in diameter.
- Outline the meat on the board at intervals with nails. Lace with string from nail to nail across the meat to hold it in place. Sharpened wooden pegs can also be nailed into the meat to hold it in place.
- Baste with oil and salt.
- Place the meat toward the fire, not too near, or the wood might catch fire.

Fish cooks rather quickly this way.

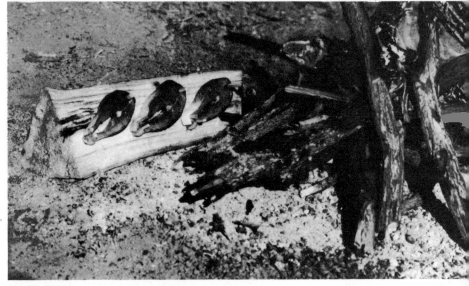

Fig.86. Salmon cooking on split logs

Fish-on-a-Stick

Tired of fish-in-a-frying-pan? Try a more natural way, with no dishes to wash afterwards.

- Clean your fish, leaving its head on.
- Sharpen both ends of a sweet-bark stick about the circumference of your finger and 6 inches longer than the fish.

- Thrust one end of the stick through the fish's mouth, up inside near the backbone, and into the flesh of the tail (fig. 87).
- Rub the fish with oil.
- Wrap foil around the exposed end of the stick to prevent it from burning (fig. 88).
- Push the free end of the stick into the ground near the fire until the fish's head nearly touches the ground.
- Push the coals toward the stick, being careful not to let them touch the stick, or it will burn (fig. 89).
- Cook for about ½ hour, or until the fish is done.

The head of the fish may scorch, may even burn a little, but you won't want to eat that part, anyway.

Fig.87. Impaling fish on a stick

Fig.88. Wrapping foil around stick to prevent its burning

Fig.89. Coals surrounding head of fish

Outdoor Grill

Steaks and other foods that are sometimes barbecued at home can also be grilled over coals.

Place a rack on rocks over coals; place steaks or other foods to be cooked on the rack. Cook until tender and done to taste (fig. 90).

(Do not use a refrigerator rack for cooking foods directly; these racks are sometimes coated with a harmful substance.)

Fig.90. Steaks on outdoor grill

Popcorn Popper

You can improvise a sturdy popcorn popper with a large flour sifter and a backpacker rack (or another kind of rack that can be elevated above the coals).

■ Pour 2 to 3 tablespoons of popcorn in the flour sifter (fig. 91).

■ Cover the sifter with foil.

■ Place the sifter on the rack, which should be from 4 to 8 inches above the coals, depending upon the intensity of the heat. Shake the sifter back and forth a bit as the popcorn warms to heat it evenly. As the popcorn heats, it will pop and fill the sifter (fig. 92). Wear asbestos gloves to prevent a burn.

Oil is not necessary in this method. The reason oil is used in popping corn in a pan is that the oil helps to heat the corn to the point of popping. With this flour-sifter method, the heat from the coals is sufficient to cause the corn to pop.

Fig.91. Pouring popcorn into flour sifter

Fig.92. Sifter filled with popped corn

Methods from *Roughing It Easy*

Besides the methods shown above, here are five cooking methods from *Roughing It Easy* demonstrating free heat (figs. 93 to 97). Arrows show the way heat circulates.

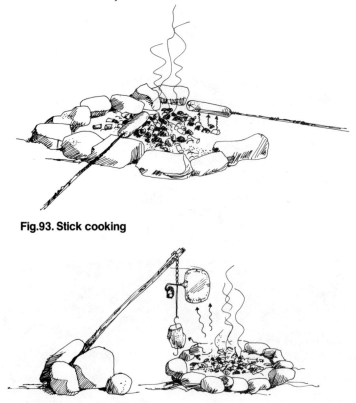

Fig.93. Stick cooking

Fig.94. Dingle-fan roaster

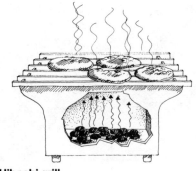

Fig.95. Hibachi grill

Fig.96. Newspaper stove rack

Fig.97. Spit

RECIPES FOR FREE HEAT

Free heat is perhaps the most popular method of cooking in the out-of-doors because it is easy and quick, with very little cleanup afterwards. Another reason for its popularity is that it is one method of cooking unique to the out-of-doors. And because it is exclusively an outdoor activity, it is especially enjoyed by the youngest of the group. Try the following recipes on your family.

Egg on a Stick

Time: 20 to 30 minutes

- With a pin or the point of a sharp
  knife, carefully tap a small hole in
  one end of   1 egg
- Sharpen to an even thickness no
  larger than 3/16 of an inch   1 small stick

Insert sharpened stick into the hole in the end and through the egg to the other end. Now carefully tap another small hole to let the stick come through.

Balance the stick on a rock near the fire so that the egg is approximately 6 inches above the coals (fig. 98). Turn in 10 to 15 minutes to cook the other side.

Fig.98. Egg on a stick

New Method for S'Mores

Method: Stick cooking
Time: 3 minutes

- Imbed (sharp end first) into the slits made by a sharp knife in the four corners of a flat side of   4 milk chocolate chips

     1 marshmallow (fig. 99)
- Repeat with   1 marshmallow
- Fit the chocolate-chip ends of the two marshmallows together (fig. 100), slide them onto the sharp end of a stick, and toast them slowly over   hot coals
- When the marshmallows are golden brown, sandwich them between   2 graham crackers (fig. 101)

This method guarantees melted chocolate, so that you will really want some more.

Fig.99. Making slits in marshmallows
to receive chocolate chips

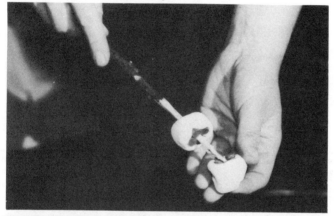

Fig.100. Fitting marshmallows and chocolate
chips together on stick

Fig.101. Marshmallows and melted chocolate
chips between graham crackers

89

Glazed Cinnamon Apple on a Stick

Method: Stick cooking

Time: 5 to 10 minutes

■ Place on the sharp end of a stick   1 apple

 Hold the apple near the flames or hot coals to scorch the peel until it bubbles (fig. 102), remove from the fire, and peel the skin off (fig. 103).

■ Roll the apple in a mixture containing sugar and cinnamon (fig. 104).

 Rotate the apple slowly over the coals until the melting sugar forms a glaze. Slice off the outer portion and eat it. Repeat dipping the apple into the sugar and cinnamon, toasting it, and eating it until the apple is gone. This will taste much like apples in apple pie.

Fig.102. Scorching the skin off an apple

Fig.103. Peeling the scorched skin

Fig.104. Rolling the apple in
sugar and cinnamon

91

Drumsticks

Method: Stick cooking
Time: 20 to 30 minutes

- Crush
- Mix together with

1 cup cornflakes
1 pound hamburger
1 egg
½ onion (chopped)
2 teaspoons salt
⅛ teaspoon pepper
1 teaspoon mustard

Wrap a small quantity of this mixture around the end of a stick, making it long instead of into a round ball. Wrap foil around the meat and part of the stick to prevent the meat from falling into the coals. Place it over a bed of coals, turning it slowly to cook it evenly. (Makes about seven drumsticks.)

CONTACT HEAT

Contact heat is like the burner on your stove. Food is placed in a container so that it may come in direct contact with the heat. Equipment used for this kind of cooking can range from pots, pans, and foil to wet paper and leaves. As kinds of food vary, so will the amount of heat and cooking time. Care should be taken not to use too many coals under items that cook better at lower heats.

Cooking in Clay

A wrapping of clay (if you are in an area where the soil is claylike) will protect food from too much heat as it cooks in a bed of coals.
- Wrap 1 inch of clay around food, such as a potato (fig. 105).
- Bury it in coals for 1 hour.
- Remove it (fig. 106), crack off the hardened clay (fig. 107), rinse the potato if necessary, and eat it immediately.

If the clay-wrapped article of food is cooked on *top* of the coals, you should double the cooking time, turning it over when half the time is up.

To hard-cook an egg, make a pinhole in its large end to relieve air pressure during the cooking. Cover the egg with clay and bury it in coals for 20 to 30 minutes. If it is placed on top of the coals, it may take as long as an hour to cook. Remember to turn it over after 30 minutes.

Cooking on Leaves

Large leaves, such as cabbage and lettuce leaves, may be used to cook meats. Be sure the leaf is edible (nonpoisonous).
- Season meat and place on leaf (fig. 108).
- Place leaf over coals.

The outside edges of the leaf will become brown and limp, but the area under the meat will remain cooler and more moist; consequently,

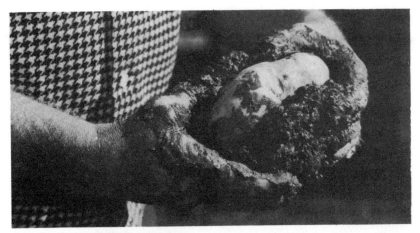

Fig.105. Covering potato with clay

Fig.106. Removing egg and potato from coals

Fig.107. Cooked egg and potato

94

Fig.108. Cooking hamburger in cabbage leaf

that part of the leaf will retain its body. Remove from coals and turn meat over to finish cooking.

Cooking in Paper

Food can be cooked in paper if it is wet before placing it on coals. Fish is the best suited for this type of cooking.
- Place oiled fish on a piece of wet paper (fig. 109). A brown paper sack works very well.
- Wet one sheet of newspaper and roll the package in it.

The size of the package and the temperature of the coals will cause the cooking time to vary (fig. 110). Ten to 15 minutes should be adequate (fig. 111). If you like this method, you may want to experiment with other foods. A paper bowl will also cook a hamburger. Set the bowl on the coals. Keep the edges of the bowl above the coals (fig. 112).

Heating Milk in Paper Cartons

Heating milk or milk products (including chocolate milk) in a pan can be a long (and sometimes not so successful) experience. Milk

Fig.109. Wrapping fish in wet paper

Fig.110. Fish cooking in wet paper

Fig.111. Cooked fish in wet paper

Fig.112. Frying hamburger in paper bowl

96

Pizza in inverted dishpan oven

Pie in inverted Dutch oven and
lid as frying pan

Colorplate 1

Stuffed green pepper

Gourmet German pancakes in Dutch oven   **Colorplate 3**

Deep-pan pizza in pie-tin oven　　　　　　　　　　　**Colorplate 4**

Heavy-duty framepack

Rucksack

Muffin-tin oven

Glazing cinnamon apple

Colorplate 6

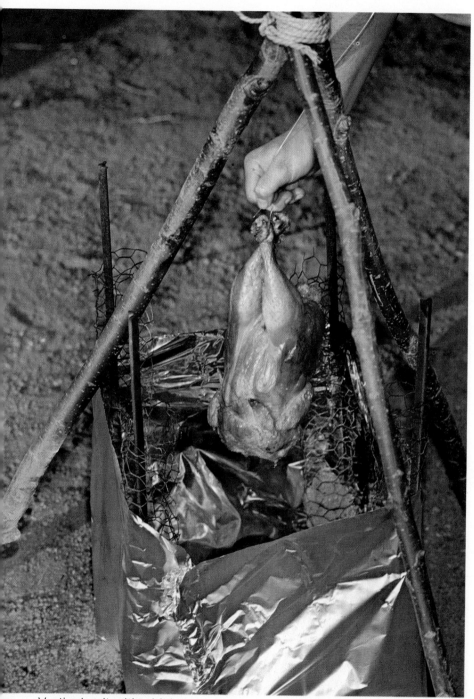

Vertical spit with chicken

Colorplate 7

Cutting fruit leather

Fruit dryer with dehydrated foods

products scorch very quickly and leave a hard-to-clean residue in the pan. Milk products purchased in non-waxed cardboard containers can be heated quickly in the carton (fig. 113).

■ Wrap foil around the bottom of the carton to prevent it from burning the seam and causing a leak.

■ Open the top of the container so that as the product heats, it will allow the steam to escape.

■ Place the carton in the coals and leave it for a few minutes. Watch closely; it heats quickly.

This method should not be used if the carton is a waxed carton.

Fig.113. Heating chocolate milk in foil-wrapped carton

Shortening-Can Cooking

One of the simplest methods of cooking with contact heat is using an empty 1-pound shortening can.

■ Place food in layers in the can, seasoning it as you go (fig. 114). (Several different kinds of vegetables may be used, along with hamburger. A suggested combination is onion, carrots, potatoes, hamburger, potatoes, carrots, and onion.)

■ Cover the top of the can with foil.

■ Place the can on medium-hot coals.

■ Put coals on top of the foil (fig. 115).

■ Cook for ½ hour to 45 minutes.

■ Using asbestos gloves, remove the can from the coals and serve a delicious meal.

Fig.114. Placing meat and vegetables in empty shortening can

Fig.115. Can covered with coals

Turnovers

Delicious turnovers can be made with English muffins:

■ Scrape out the center of both sides of an English muffin with a fork or spoon, taking care not to scrape a hole in the bun (fig. 116).

■ Fill one half of the muffin with your favorite sandwich or dessert filling (fig. 117).

Suggestions:

Sandwich:	egg salad
	cheese
	deviled ham with pickles
	diced Spam with pickles and salad dressing
	ham and cheese
Dessert:	cherry
	peach
	apple
	other (try your own)

■ Cover the filled half of the muffin with the other half and butter both on the outside (fig. 118).

■ Wrap the muffin with foil, using the drugstore-wrap method below.

■ Place it in coals for 3 to 5 minutes per side.

Drugstore Wrap

■ Cut two pieces of lightweight foil or one piece of heavy-duty foil twice the circumference of the item to be wrapped.

■ Place the food in the middle of the shiny side of one piece of foil. (Tests have proven that the shiny side of the foil reflects more radiant heat.)

■ Bring the opposite sides of the foil together and fold their ends over together ½ inch at a time, turning them down in small folds until they can be folded no longer.

■ Flatten the top of the package and roll each open edge toward the center in small folds. The edges of the package must be tightly sealed. This is called the drugstore wrap.

■ If the package needs to be wrapped again, place the folded top of the package downward in the center of the other piece of foil and fold.

Fig.116. Scraping center out of muffin

Fig.117. Filling one-half of muffin
with cherry-pie filling

Fig.118. Buttering turnover

100

Tin-Can Stove with Frying Pan

Anything you can cook in a pan at home can be cooked this way. This is very good to use outside when the gas or electricity goes out.

- In a #10 can cut with tin snips a door 4 inches tall and 3 inches wide (if you cut it wider than 3 inches, the base of the can will not be strong enough to support the pan on the top of the stove). This stove is not designed to support a lot of weight. It is best for cooking for two or three.
- Cut out the top of the can (fig. 119). Punch about six holes around the top backside of the can for ventilation (use a punch-type can opener).
- For the flame inside the can, use a buddy burner and a damper (described in *Roughing It Easy;* we will discuss it briefly here.) The buddy burner is simply a corrugated piece of cardboard the height of a tuna-fish can rolled to fit inside the empty, clean can. A piece of paraffin wax is melted down into the cardboard. The damper is the lid of the tuna-fish can attached with wire to the end of a bent clothes hanger. (The wire is thrust through holes in the tuna-can lid to secure the end of the clothes hanger to the lid.) Small pieces of wood or other types of burnable materials can be used under the can as well.
- Soap the outside of the pan, then cover it with foil for good measure to keep the pan from being blackened with smoke (fig. 120). Wax tends to give off a lot of smoke, so the can is usually used only once.
- Set the pan on the top of the tin-can stove and fry your favorite camp food (fig. 121).

Earmuff Toast

Light bread such as that purchased at the grocery store can be toasted on the side of the #10 can when it is warm. On a cold morning, your hands will be warmed as you hold the toast to the side of the can.

- When the can is warm, take two slices of bread and place them on opposite sides of the can. Place them just behind the oven door and roll the bread on with your hands.

Fig.119. Tin-can stove and fuel

Fig.120. Wrapping frying pan with foil

Fig.121. Food cooking on stove

102

- Usually, after you have held the bread for a moment, it will stick to the outside of the can.
- With a stick or a knife, pop the bread off when it has browned.
- To toast the other side of the bread, turn it over on the can (fig. 122). If the bread is too light, it may compact the bread to toast both sides.

Fig.122. Earmuff toast

Methods from *Roughing It Easy*

Again we turn to *Roughing It Easy* for examples (besides those shown above) of the contact-heat principle (figs. 123 to 130).

Fig.124. Food cooking in foil in pit

Fig.123. Food cooking on tin can

Fig.126. Food cooking in Dutch oven

Fig.125. Water heating in paper cup over coals

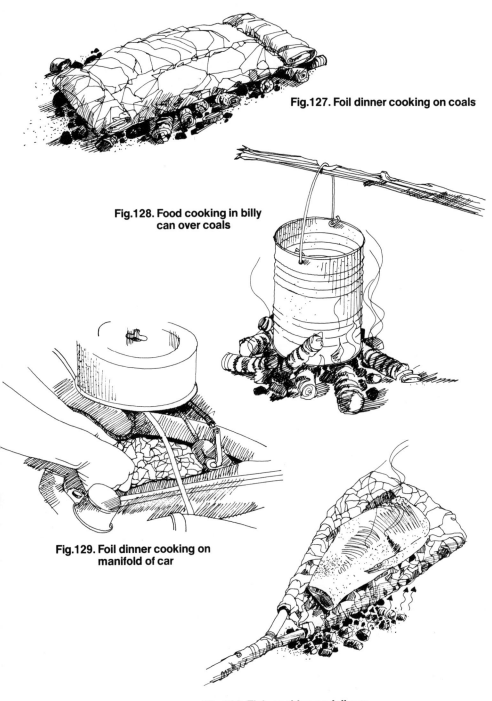

Fig.127. Foil dinner cooking on coals

Fig.128. Food cooking in billy can over coals

Fig.129. Foil dinner cooking on manifold of car

Fig.130. Fish cooking on foil pan

105

RECIPES FOR CONTACT HEAT

Ways of cooking in the open with contact heat are almost endless, and so are recipes. Among the new recipes here are old favorites with perhaps a twist or two for more lip-smacking goodness.

Orange, Egg, and Muffin Breakfast

Method: Contact heat
Time: 15 to 20 minutes
- Cut in half and
  remove meat
  from both
  halves of   1 orange (fig. 131)
- Break into one
  half   1 egg
- In the other
  half, place   Batter for 1 muffin (fig. 132)

Place each half-orange on foil large enough to bring to the top and twist.

Place the foil-wrapped orange in hot coals for the required 15 to 20 minutes.

Hush Puppies

Method: Dutch oven
Time: 1 to 2 minutes on each side.
- Sift together   1 cup cornmeal
                  1 tablespoon flour
                  1 teaspoon baking powder
                  1 teaspoon salt
- Add   ¼ cup finely diced onion
                  ½ chopped green pepper
- Into the above
  stir   1 egg, well beaten
                  ⅓ cup milk

Form little balls with this batter and drop them into hot oil (just short of smoking stage). Keep turning them until they are brown. Remove the hush puppies and drain on paper towels. (Serves four.)

Fig.131. Removing orange from peel with thumb

Fig.132. Orange, egg, and muffin breakfast

TV Dinner

Method: Wet newspapers and foil
Time: 20 to 35 minutes

- When coals are hot, wet two layers of newspaper
- Center on the long side of the wet newspaper 1 TV dinner

Fold wet newspaper over the TV dinner and roll up the ends (fig. 133). Place the dinner on a bed of coals and cover with hot coals (fig. 134). The wet newspaper will keep the dinner from scorching. After about ½ hour, enjoy a delicious meal (fig. 135).

Fig.133. Wrapping a TV dinner in wet newspaper

Fig.134. Hot coals over wet newspaper dinner

Fig.135. Hot TV dinner

Plastic-Bag Breakfast

Method: Plastic bag
Time: 3 to 4 minutes

- Break into a
plastic
Zip-Lock bag
and seal   1 egg
- Place plastic
bag in   pan of boiling water (fig. 136).

Variations: Any foods that have been precooked are suited to this method of cooking. For extra protection, use double bags.

Fig.136. Egg cooking in Zip-Lock plastic bag

Fig.137. Cooked egg

Mixed-Vegetable Foil Dinner

Method: Heavy-duty foil
Time: 10 to 15 minutes per side

- On one piece
  of foil place   1 to 2 slices of a large onion
- Shape a patty
  from   ¼ pound hamburger
- With the patty,
  place on piece
  of foil   1 teaspoon dry gravy mix
       seasoned salt and pepper
       ⅓ cup mixed vegetables (from can)
       ⅓ cup sliced white potatoes (from can)
- Optional   1 teaspoon dry gravy over top
       1 slice of large onion

Wrap in foil (shiny side in), using drugstore-wrap method, and cook on coals or grill until done. Serves one.

Broasted Corn

Method: Contact heat
Time: 15 to 20 minutes

- Carefully pull
  back husk and
  remove silk
  and any
  foreign matter
  by washing   1 ear of corn
- While corn is
  still wet,
  sprinkle lightly
  with   salt

    Replace husk so that no corn is exposed and place it on a hot bed

Fig.138. Corn roasting

of coals (fig. 138), turning it one-fourth the way around every 3 to 5 minutes (can also be wrapped in foil).

Remove the husk, butter the corn, and eat it immediately.

For a faster way of broasting corn, simply toss fresh-picked corn (in the husk) into the fire. Bury it in coals for five minutes. Remove from coals and open to remove silk. Butter and salt it to taste.

Puffed Potatoes

Method: Skillet or Dutch oven
Time: 15 to 20 minutes
- Mix together   1 cup mashed potatoes (may use rehydrated potatoes)
  1 cup flour
  ⅓ cup milk
  2 teaspoons baking powder
  1 teaspoon salt
- Drop mixture
  by spoonfuls
  into   hot grease (2 inches deep)
  Brown on both sides. Makes 15 to 20 small puffs.

Quick Scones

Method: Dutch oven or frying pan
Time: 3 to 5 minutes
- Place in pan to
  heat   ½ pound (2 cups) shortening or oil
- Cut in half   1 English muffin
- (Or: cut in
  quarters   1 slice bread (slightly dry)
- With a fork dip
  muffin or
  bread pieces
  into   basic pancake batter

Drop these into hot oil. Usually, when a wooden match ignites in the oil, it is hot enough to cook the scones. When they are golden

112

Fig.139. Quick scones browning

brown, turn them and let them brown on the other side (fig. 139). Serve plain or roll scones in sugar and cinnamon or powdered sugar, or spread with honey, jam, jelly, or syrup.

Brighten-Up Breakfast Stew

Method: Dutch oven or kettle
Time: Method 1: 10 to 15 minutes; Method 2: 20 minutes, if potatoes are cooked

Preparation Method 1 (fast and easy):
- Slice in small
  pieces and fry ½ pound bacon
- Drain away
  most of the
  bacon grease.
  Cube and add 1 can potatoes (29 ounces)
- Salt and
  pepper
  potatoes to
  taste.
- Scramble and
  fry in separate
  pan
- Add eggs to
  mixture   6 eggs
- Season as desired.
-

Note: Diced ham or Spam can be substituted for the bacon.
Serves four to six people.

Preparation Method 2:
- Boil, peel, and
  cube   4 medium potatoes
- Slice in pieces
  and fry   ½ pound bacon
- Drain off most
  of the grease.

114

Add cubed
potatoes and
salt and
pepper to
taste. Fry until
potatoes are
browned.
- Add and
  scramble
  together   6 eggs

Add more salt and pepper if necessary. When eggs are cooked, serve plain or with catsup.

Sheepherder's Stew

Method: Dutch oven or kettle
Time: 35 minutes
- Chop up either
  fresh or
  cooked   beef
- (or use   1 pound ground beef)
- If meat is
  fresh, brown it
  and add   ½ teaspoon salt
                   4 diced raw potatoes
                   carrots (2 to 3 peeled and diced)
                   ½ diced onion
- Season with   1 teaspoon salt
- Add   2 cans cream of mushroom soup
                   ½ can (soup size) milk

Cook ingredients over low heat until vegetables and meat are tender (25 minutes).
- Add if desired 1 can beans
                  1 can liquid-packed corn

Cook an additional 10 minutes to heat precooked vegetables. Serves six to eight people.

Stuffed Green Pepper

Method: Foil
Time: 30 minutes
- Mix together   ½ pound hamburger
                  salt and pepper to taste
                  (Optional: 1 egg and 1 diced onion)
- Stuff mixture
  into   4 green peppers

  Place peppers on shiny side of individual pieces of foil and wrap with drugstore wrap. Place over coals and cook 12 to 15 minutes on each side.

Foil Ham and Cheese Rolls

Method: Foil
Time: 10 to 15 minutes
- Cut gashes 1
  inch apart
  across the top
  of   hard dinner rolls
- Mix together
  the following   1 can deviled ham
                  ¼ cup diced sweet pickles
                  ⅛ teaspoon garlic salt
- Spread this
  mixture
  generously
  inside each
  gash
- Insert inside
  each gash   1 piece of cheese
- Sprinkle top
  with   Parmesan cheese (optional)

  Wrap each in foil and place in coals for 10 minutes or until warmed through.

Fruit Fritters

Method: Skillet or tin-can stove
- Make a batter
  with
    1 egg
    1 teaspoon baking powder
    ¾ cup flour
    ¼ teaspoon salt
    ½ cup milk
- Dip into batter
  and fry any of
  the following
  sliced
    apples
    bananas
    oranges

Roll in powdered sugar. Use these as appetizers or snacks.

Mexically Sally ("Eat-with-a-Fork Tacos")

Method: Skillet
Time: 15 minutes
- Fry in a large
  skillet
    1 pound ground beef
    ½ onion, chopped
- Drain away
  grease and
  add
    Large can of chili beans (30 ounces)
- Continue
  cooking until
  well heated.
- Slice in small
  pieces and do
  not combine
    ½ head of lettuce
    3 tomatoes
- Grate   ½ pound of cheese
- Place on plate 1 handful of tortilla chips
- Open   1 can taco sauce

Serve on plate in the following order: tortilla chips, meat and beans, lettuce, cheese, taco sauce.

Chicken with Rice

Method: Dutch oven

Time: About 45 minutes

- In oiled Dutch
  oven, brown   pieces of chicken
- Sprinkle with   salt and pepper
- Combine   2 10½-ounce cans of cream of chicken soup
  1 cup instant rice

- And spoon
  over chicken.
- Sprinkle with   ½ cup Parmesan cheese

Place Dutch oven on coals and cover lid with coals. Bake until done.

SOLAR HEAT

Solar heat box cooking is becoming more popular every day. Try your hand at making a solar reflector stove and/or a solar oven. You'll be excited with the results.

SOLAR REFLECTOR

A stove made of paper sounds about as practical as a pitcher carved from ice, but that is going to be our project. Constructed almost entirely from cardboard, this reflector cooker will broil steaks, grill hot dogs, fry bacon and eggs, and make hotcakes and coffee. It will also heat the water for doing the dishes. All that is necessary is clear weather, because this stove cooks with sunshine! (fig. 140.)

Fig.140. Solar reflector cooker

Stop to think about it for a minute and you'll remember that every time we cook—whether it is with gas, electricity, or charcoal—we indirectly use the sun's energy, which has been stored up and reconverted to heat. Basically, then, our solar stove's fuel for cooking goes back many years. Sun-dried foods have long been eaten, and crude solar stoves were built a century ago. Besides, who hasn't heard of cooking an egg on the sidewalk on a really hot day?

Materials

Cardboard—as required

Poster board—six sheets, 22 x 28 inches

Aluminum foil—one roll heavy-duty, 18 x 37

Plywood—one piece, 18 x 24 inches

¾-inch aluminum tubing—approximately 64 inches

¾-inch mounting flange—one

Grill—one

Curtain rod—one

Broomstick—4 feet

Clothesline—1 foot

Glue—as required

Masking tape—as required

3/16-x-1-inch bolt with wingnut—one set

The reflector framework is cut from cardboard, approximately 3/16 inch thick, the kind large cartons are made from. Some poster board and aluminum foil will complete the cooker itself. A grill (for hot dogs, hamburgers, or pans) is made from plywood, some tubing, and an inexpensive hand grill that costs about 50 cents.

Study the plans first to get the overall picture and to see how much new material will be needed.

The other items will be easy to find. Get all the materials ready and then begin construction. An eager beaver can do the job in a day or so and begin sampling outdoor cooking à la sun right away.

A word about the principle of our reflector cooker will be helpful before we proceed any further. The sun above simply focuses onto the bottom of the grill all the sun's rays that strike its surface. Even on a clear winter day the 12 square feet of area in our cooker collect a lot of "warmth" which, when shrunk into the 1-foot area at the grill, becomes concentrated "heat."

Giant solar furnaces use curved reflectors. They generate thousands of degrees of heat at their focal points, using the same principle. To do this they must be very accurately made and of parabolic shape.

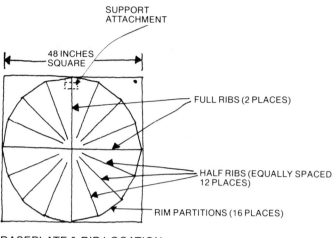

SUPPORT
ATTACHMENT

48 INCHES
SQUARE

FULL RIBS (2 PLACES)

HALF RIBS (EQUALLY SPACED
12 PLACES)

RIM PARTITIONS (16 PLACES)

BASEPLATE & RIB LOCATION

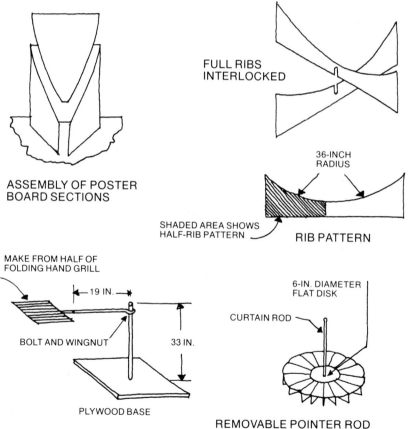

FULL RIBS
INTERLOCKED

ASSEMBLY OF POSTER
BOARD SECTIONS

36-INCH
RADIUS

SHADED AREA SHOWS
HALF-RIB PATTERN

RIB PATTERN

MAKE FROM HALF OF
FOLDING HAND GRILL

19 IN.

BOLT AND WINGNUT

33 IN.

PLYWOOD BASE

6-IN. DIAMETER
FLAT DISK

CURTAIN ROD

REMOVABLE POINTER ROD
AND CENTER DISK INSTALLATION

Fig.141. Plans for solar reflector cooker

121

This specially shaped curve reflects all the rays onto one tiny spot and gives the furnace a concentration ratio of many thousands to one. Obviously, we don't want such high temperatures, for they would melt our pans!

Our reflector will use a radius of 36 inches instead of a true parabolic curve. This results in a larger spot at the focal point. And, instead of one bowl-shaped reflector, we will use a number of wedge-shaped sections. Thus our focal point will be roughly the size of the cooking pan, which is just what we want. This model can be scaled down, but the heat will not be so intense.

Instructions
- First, cut a base piece 4 feet square from the 3/16-inch cardboard.
- Mark the layout of the reflector ribs right on this base (fig. 142). With a pencil and a piece of string, draw a 48-inch-diameter circle. This is the size our finished cooker will be. Next draw two lines through the center of the base, perpendicular to each other as shown on the plans. These mark the location of the main ribs, which we will make next.
- Draw two main ribs from a piece 12 x 48 inches. Cut these carefully, using a sharp linoleum knife, a pocketknife, or a modeler's razor knife. Be sure to plan ahead so that you will not waste material as you lay out the ribs. Each of the main ribs has a notch at the center. Notice that one is on the top and one on the bottom so that they will interlock.
- Using a full rib as a pattern, mark out 12 half-ribs. Before cutting these, cement the full ribs to the base plate on the lines previously drawn. Model airplane glue or a good household cement will work well. Use straight pins to hold the ribs down and in place (fig. 143). Remove the pins when cement is dry. While the parts are drying, cut out the remaining ribs.
- Three half-ribs fit between the quarter-sections of the circle. Glue these in place, lining up the end of each one with the circle you drew on the base plate.
- While the half-ribs are drying, cut the rectangular filler pieces of cardboard. These rim partitions fit between the outer tips of the ribs to complete the framework. These pieces should be 12 inches high and approximately 9 to 9¼ inches wide. Each opening should be measured for proper fit. Fit each square together and tape the seams (fig. 144).
- When the framework is thoroughly dry, cut the wedge-shaped pieces of poster board. (Since these form the curve that will reflect the sun's rays, use poster board that is thin enough to bend easily, yet has

Fig.142. Base with glued-on coardboard ribs

Fig.143. Pins used to hold ribs in place

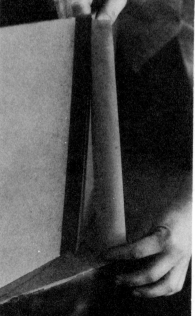

Fig.144. Taping seams

123

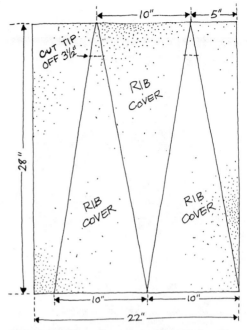

Fig.145. Marking rib covers on poster board

sufficient body to hold the proper shape. Lighter cardboard would have a tendency to ripple and wave.) By marking a piece of poster board as shown (fig. 145), you will be able to get three rib covers from each sheet 22 x 28 inches. Now cut 3½ inches off the tip to help the center fit better. Do not cement this in place yet; it will be the pattern for 15 more pieces. Cut them carefully, making sure they will cover any of the spaces between the ribs. (In spite of care, there may be slight inaccuracies in the framework.) It is better to have the poster-board pieces a bit too large than too small.

■ Begin to cement the cut pieces into place. Since butting the joints smoothly against each other would be difficult, glue eight pieces in alternate spaces first (fig. 146). Spread glue along the tops of two ribs and the intervening filler piece, then lay the poster-board wedge in place and carefully press down so that it touches the ribs at all points. The glue will dry well enough in a minute or two so that you can go on to the next piece. Don't forget to leave every other section open.

■ Cover the open spaces with the remaining eight pieces of poster board by running a bead of cement along their edges. These eight pieces will of course lap over the edges of the pieces already glued in place, thus making a strong point. If you run into difficulty at the center

124

where all the points come together, simply trim them off an inch or two. The hole left can later be covered with a separate piece of poster board. Running masking tape along the seams will make a better glue joint and will hold the piece tight while it is drying (fig. 147).

■ Cut a 6-inch circle out of poster board and glue it over the center hole; tape the edges for reinforcement (fig. 148). The reflector is now ready for application of the aluminum foil that will give it the mirror-like finish necessary for collecting heat for cooking.

■ Cut out 16 pieces of smooth-surfaced aluminum foil—the kind used in the kitchen for wrapping food. These should be slightly larger than the poster-board pieces to assure complete coverage of the reflector surface. Use rubber cement to stick the foil to the poster board, and be sure to have the shiny side up (fig. 149). Work carefully and try to keep the foil smooth, but don't worry if the finished job is not perfect. The cooker shown in the illustrations has a few ripples but works well anyway.

■ Install a marker for the focal point of the reflector so that you will know where to place the grill for the fastest cooking. This is simply a small, inexpensive curtain rod of the type used on kitchen doors (fig. 150). It consists of two tubes, one fitted inside the other. Cut a short length of the larger tube and insert it into a hole punched in the center of the reflector. Better still, use a drill the same size as the tube or slightly smaller to give a snug fit. Now cement the tube in place. The smaller tube will fit into this "holder" and can be removed for easier handling when not needed.

■ As we mentioned before, the focal distance from our reflector is the proper place for mounting our grill. With a spherical reflector the focal length is half the radius, or in this case, 18 inches. As a double check, aim the reflector at the sun and adjust the tilt until there is no shadow visible from the pointer rod. Then hold a piece of wrapping paper with a small hole punched in it right at the tip of the pointer. Move the paper toward the reflector and then away from it until the smallest spot is observed on the paper. This is the actual focal point, and the pointer rod should be cut to this length.

■ For support attachments, cut out two squares (2 x 2 inches) and one rectangle (2 x 6 inches) of cardboard as shown by the dotted lines on the plans and cement them to the center top back of the cardboard base. The squares go first, and then the rectangle. After these are well dried, run a short length of clothesline through the slot and tie the ends in a square knot. Drill holes through a 48-inch length of 1-inch dowel

Fig.146. Alternating wedges glued onto ribs

Fig.147. Gluing and taping wedges

(broomstick or tubing), spacing the holes about an inch apart halfway down the dowel (fig. 151). Insert a nail to engage the loop of clothesline. You can now set up the reflector so that it will stand alone.

■ To make the grill, first cut a plywood base 18 by 24 inches. Any thickness from ½ to 1 inch will do. Mark the center and install a mounting flange for the ¾-inch aluminum-tubing vertical support, which is 40 inches long, as shown in the plans.

Fig.148. Gluing circle over center hole

Fig.149. Gluing foil to wedges

■ The adjustable arm is also aluminum tubing, 24 inches long. Flatten one end as shown and bend around a piece of pipe or a broomstick to make the collar, which fits over the vertical support. Drill a 3/16-inch hole as shown and insert a bolt and a wingnut. The other end of the adjustable arm may now be flattened. Be careful to keep the flat area at right angles to the collar so that the grill will be horizontal when installed.

Fig.150. Stick bracing solar reflector

Fig.151. Skillet on griddle

- Slide the grill in place, and the solar cooker is complete.
- Positioning the reflector is simple if you follow these directions. Stand behind it and face it right at the sun. Tilt it back until the shadow of the pointer rod vanishes as it did when we checked for focal length. This means that the reflector is aimed perfectly and that all the sun's rays will be bounced right where we want them.
- Holding the reflector in this position, slip the dowel or broomstick through the rope loop and put the nail through the hole just below the loop. With the reflector on its own feet you can now put the grill in place.
- Loosen the wingnut on the adjustable arm and move it up or down until the grill rests just above the tip of the pointer rod. As a double check, pass your hand quickly just above the grill. It should be hot, ready for you to start cooking.

How to Use Your Solar Cooker

- The grill surface itself is fine for cooking hot dogs, burgers, or steaks. Grease will drip onto the reflector but will not harm it.
- For bacon and eggs, hotcakes, and the like, place a skillet on the

griddle. And if you like your steaks seared quickly to keep in the juice, use the skillet for them, too. By putting it on the grill a few minutes early you can store up extra heat that will cook the steak more rapidly.

■ Water can be heated in a kettle or pot. To get the maximum efficiency from your solar cooker, use blackened utensils; however, just about any kind of utensil works satisfactorily. For variety try using a pressure cooker.

■ Because the sun moves across the sky, the position of the reflector will be different as time passes. In the early morning or late afternoon it will be nearly vertical, while at noon you will have to place it practically flat on the ground. That's why you drilled so many holes in the support rod. If you plan to boil beans or make stew, occasional adjustment of the reflector will be required to keep the hot spot where it will do the most good. The shadow from the pointer rod is the thing to watch. For bacon and eggs, hot dogs, and even steak, one setting will usually do the trick.

■ After cooking your meal and washing the dishes, remove the grill from the aluminum tube and clean it, too. Then wipe off the reflector surface with a paper towel or damp cloth, and that's all there is to the job of solar cooking.

Advantages of Solar Cooking

Of course, solar stoves won't take the place of other kinds of cooking all the time. When the sun goes down, you had better be through cooking, and on a rainy day, the reflector is not much use except maybe to crawl under to keep dry! But properly used in clear weather, it will amaze the most skeptical observer. Here are a few of the advantages of solar cooking:

■ As you discovered when you held your hand close to the focal point, there is no warming-up period with a solar stove—it is hot right away! By the time the fellow with the charcoal brazier gets a good bed of coals, you will be doing the dishes.

■ Besides, he paid for his fuel, while yours was free for the taking.

■ And solar energy is available anywhere the sun shines—mountains, desert, beach, or your own back yard.

■ You will have noticed how nice it is not to have your eyes full of smoke.

130

- Solar cooking is cool cooking, too, because the heat goes into the food on the grill and doesn't roast the person doing the cooking.
- You won't need matches to get your cooker going.
- There's no danger of setting anything on fire, either.
- There are no ashes or soot to contend with. And if someone complains about the lack of that charcoal or hickory taste, provide him with a bottle of liquid smoke.

Seriously, you will have a lot of fun cooking with sunshine. It's safe, it's clean, and it's free. Chances are you'll like it enough to want a portable cooker for the next camping trip, so that you won't be tied down to a fireplace and the bother that goes with it. So, save up for a commercial folding cooker, or put your ingenuity to work and make a version of the cardboard stove that is portable.

THE SOLAR OVEN

The "greenhouse" effect is well known to those who grow plants in such structures and also to those of us who have left the windows of a car rolled up on a warm, sunshiny day. The rays of the sun go through the glass well enough, but the reflections of longer wavelength are unable to bounce back out of the car. The result is aptly described as resembling an oven. And that is just what you can build—a solar oven that will do a good job of cooking on a clear day, even in winter.

One aim of solar scientists is to provide a means of cooking for those countries in which fuel is scarce or expensive. Dr. Maria Telkes designed such an oven, which she feels might be mass-produced at a reasonable price. Our design is copied from the Telkes oven, which has been demonstrated in foreign lands.

Basically, the solar oven consists of a box for the food and a glass cover to admit and trap heat inside the box (fig. 152). The box shown is made from galvanized iron but could well have been aluminum for lighter weight. The reflector panels are of aluminum.

You will need the sheet-metal parts, a piece of double-strength window glass, a sealing strip for the glass, and three handles. The box is insulated with spun glass material 2 inches thick for greater heat retention.

Materials

28-gauge galvanized iron—16 square feet

No. 6, ⅜-inch sheet-metal screws—approximately 24

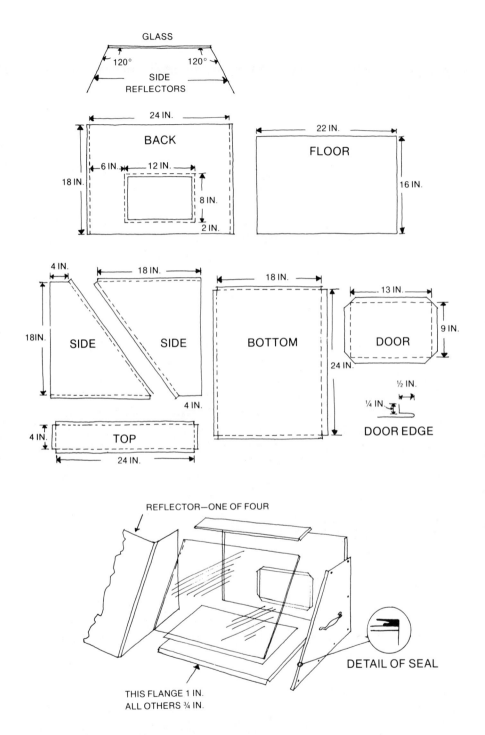

Fig.152. Plans for solar oven

2-inch fiberglass insulation—12 square feet
Double-strength window glass—22 x 24 inches
Drawer pulls—3
Flat black paint—one spray can
2-inch roofing nails—six
Sealer strip—8 feet of ⅛″ x 1″ felt weather stripping or similar material
Aluminum sheet .025 x 22 by 24 inches—four pieces

Again, it is a good idea to have all materials on hand before beginning the project. One exception might be the sheet metal for the box, in case you decide to let your local sheet-metal shop do the cutting and bending for you. Unless you are familiar with metalwork, having it done will result in a more professional job at little additional cost.

Instructions

If you want to do all the work yourself, and feel that you can handle the job, this is the way to begin.

■ The bottom of the oven is a rectangle of metal, with the corners notched out to allow bending up flanges all around the sides. These flanges are ¾ inch, and are bent up 90 degrees, except for the front edge, which is a closed 45-degree angle, 1 inch long, as shown in the drawing.

■ The right and left side panels may be cut from one rectangle of metal to save material. Lay them out carefully to prevent waste. Again, flanges are bent ¾ inch wide at the front and top. The back and bottom edges are left flat. Be sure to make the bends opposite on each part so that you will have a right-hand panel and a left-hand panel, and not two of a kind!

■ The oven back has ¾-inch flanges on each side and an opening cut in it for the door. Notch the corners of the opening 45 degrees and bend the ½-inch stiffener flanges in the same direction as the side flanges. This will strengthen the door opening and also give the back a finished appearance.

■ Now make the top of the box. This is a channel with one flange at 90 degrees to fit the back and the other flange to 45 degrees to match the slope of the glass. Next come two retaining angles 18 inches long, with ¾-x-1-inch legs. The box is now complete except for the door.

■ The door is the only difficult part to make; care must be taken to bend it correctly. The double, or "hemmed" edge strengthens the door, and the flange left standing will fit into the opening in the back of the box. A snug fit here will make for a neat, effective door that will seal properly and help keep the heat inside where we want it.

■ A false bottom is needed to prevent collapsing of the insulation under the weight of the food. It is a rectangle of metal sized as shown in the drawing. Make sure it is not so large that it contacts the front, sides, or back of the box. This would cause heat loss by conduction to those parts.

It might be well to mention here that an alternate method of construction can be used, employing a little ingenuity and the do-it-yourself aluminum sheets and angles available at the hardware store. This method uses flat sheets, with angles attached to them instead of flanges bent from the sheets themselves. Of course, the 45-degree angles would have to be eliminated, and a slightly different sealing technique used for the glass, but some builders may prefer doing it this way.

Now, with the metal parts formed either in the sheet-metal shop or at your own workbench, you are ready to begin assembly of the oven.

■ The simplest way to put the oven together is with sheet-metal screws. Use ⅜-inch No. 6 screws for this purpose. They are available at the sheet-metal shop, or your hardware store. If you are using aluminum, substitute hardened aluminum screws, since different metals coming in contact with each other may cause a corrosive action.

■ Mark pencil guidelines ⅜-inch from the bottom edge of the side panels, spaced as shown on the drawing. Center-punch the holes and drill with a No. 40 drill. A hand drill is fine; an electric drill is even better for this purpose. Now, with the bottom of the oven on a flat surface, hold the side panel against it and in its proper place. Drill through the holes in the side panel and on into the flange of the bottom. It is a good idea to put in a screw as each hole is drilled to insure perfect alignment and prevent shifting of the parts. Notice that the bottom flange overlaps the side but no holes are drilled at this point.

■ With both side panels attached to the bottom, the back of the box may now be put in place and holes drilled. Continue to insert screws as holes are drilled, carefully keeping the parts lined up as you progress.

The oven is taking shape by now, and needs only the top to be added. Before you do this, however, you must install the glass in the front of the box. Needless to say, care must be taken during this operation so that the glass will not be broken. Don't cut your fingers on the edges.

■ Clean the glass carefully with water. Then glue on the sealing strip around the edge with a good cement (Goodyear Pliobond works well), following the directions to insure a strong joint. If you are able to find a sealer that fits over the edge of the glass, the job will be easy.

■ When the sealing strip is attached and properly "set," the glass may be put in place in the oven. Slide it down through the top, which you have left open for this purpose. For this operation lay the oven on its front face, making sure you have a perfectly flat surface to work on.

■ Next install the 18-inch angles that hold the glass in place. Carefully drill holes in the sides of the box as shown on the drawing, locating them so that they will match the angles when they are put in position. Slip the angles through the opening in the top and set them on the glass with the 1-inch leg flat against the side of the box.

■ Working from the top, or reaching through the opening in the back of the box, press one angle very lightly against the glass. Do not force the glass so that it flattens the sealing strip, because this strip acts as a cushion to prevent breakage of the glass, in addition to its sealing function. While holding the angle, mark through the holes in the side to indicate the proper location for the holes in the angle. Remove the angle, drill holes in it, then replace and insert a sheet-metal screw.

■ Repeat this process on the other side.

■ With the glass installed, the top may be put on and holes drilled through it and into the back and sides. Notice that the top fits over the back and side panels.

■ The oven is now complete except for the carrying handles on each side and a similar handle on the door. These are attached with screws.

■ Fit the door into the opening and mark the holes for the turn-buttons that hold the door tight. Drill 3/16-inch holes in the back panel, and install the turn-buttons with nuts, bolts, and washers. The washers hold the buttons away from the metal so they will clear the hemmed edge of the door.

■ The spun-glass insulation is now cut to proper shape with a sharp knife or linoleum cutter. Use a straightedge for accurate trimming. Plan carefully so as not to waste material. The bottom piece can be leveled 45 degrees at the front if care is taken.

■ Paint the inside surfaces of the insulation with flat black enamel. For convenience, use spray paint.

■ After the paint is dry, the insulation is glued into the box with Pliobond or its equivalent. To do this, remove the back of the box and set it aside. Positioning the oven with the glass down, cement the top insulation in place first and allow to dry. Tip the box right side up and cement the bottom insulation in place. Press five 2-inch roofing nails point-down into the insulation and lay the false bottom over them.

■ This bottom piece is painted flat black, too.

■ The side insulation can now be cemented into place, and the box is complete except for the back.

■ Cement insulation to the back panel, cut the small rectangle from the opening and place it on the inside of the door.

■ The back may now be carefully replaced and the screws inserted.

■ Put in an óven thermometer, fasten the door in place, and you are ready for the reflector panels, which are hinged to the box as shown in the drawing.

In tests the box itself will reach an inner temperature of only about 250 degrees. The reason is' that heat loss to the surrounding air prevents the temperature inside from climbing higher. If we could increase the amount of heat going into the box, the oven would get

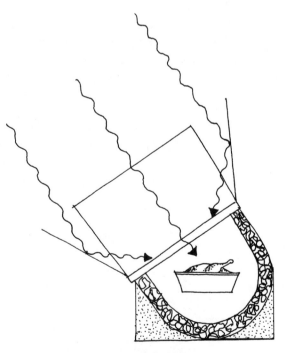

**Fig.153. Solar oven angled to
receive rays of sun**

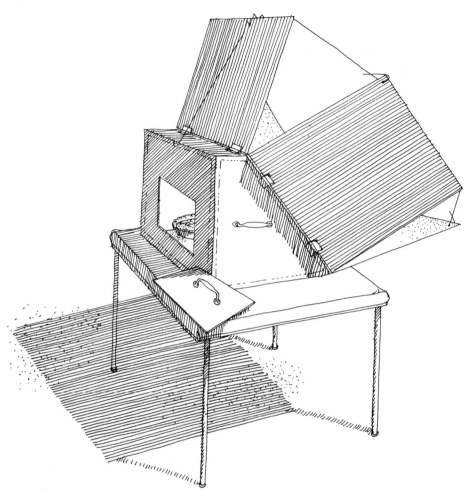

Fig.154. Pie baking in solar oven

hotter. For this reason we add the aluminum reflector plates. Use Alclad if it is available.

■ Rivet two hinges to each reflector. Be sure to have two reflectors hinged on the ends and two hinged on the sides. If the Alclad sheets have red lettering on one side, use the opposite side for the reflecting surface. Attach the hinges to the box with sheet-metal screws, installing the bottom reflector, then the sides, and finally the top. Besides their primary purpose, the reflectors also protect the glass.

■ An angle of 30 degrees to the received rays of the sun will reflect them into the box, so we open the side panels to this angle. We face the oven directly toward the sun, and thus this angle will always suffice for the side reflectors. The 45-degree tilt of the glass is a compromise angle that gives all-around performance. However, a little thought will tell us that for maximum performance the angle of the top and bottom reflectors will vary with the position of the sun in the sky (fig. 153).

■ Adjusting the oven is simpler than it sounds. Set it out in the sun, preferably on a wooden table, and face it toward the sun. Open all the reflectors. Now swing the top reflector up and down while watching the inside of the oven. You will be able to tell when you have it at the proper angle by the reflection of the sun's rays on the dull black insulation.

■ Bend the end of a piece of galvanized wire to act as a stop, insert this wire in a hole in the top reflector, and wrap the free end around the loosened screw as shown in the illustration (fig. 154).

■ Swing the side reflectors into position, checking the angle they make with the glass by means of a cardboard template. Using two wires, attach them to the top reflector. Now swing the bottom reflector up, watching the inside of the oven again. When it is properly positioned, fix two wires in place from the bottom reflector to the side reflectors, and the oven is ready.

The oven will reach a temperature of 350°F. in 15 minutes. This was tested in Arizona in mid-January, when the air temperature was in the low 60s. The first time it was used, it baked a loaf of bread in just over an hour, and then cooked a 3-pound roast in 3½ hours! A whole meal can be cooked in the solar oven.

LIGHTWEIGHT CAMPING

Lightweight camping provides many advantages for anyone with an urge to backpack into the wilderness, hike across the dusty desert, ski cross-country in the freezing cold of winter, bicycle off the beaten path, canoe, or challenge the high mountains.

Perhaps the greatest joy of lightweight camping springs from that rediscovered sense of privacy and oneness with nature. You'll find yourself much more dependent on the elements, and in a situation that involves more responsibility—both for yourself and the ecology of the land. There is a physical joy, too, in testing your own abilities and meeting your own goals. And if you travel with others, close ties of companionship will develop as you travel and work together. Finally, you'll be able to see and live in country inaccessible to the automobile camper. The key to any successful trip is to know where you are going and how to return.

EASY-TO-CARRY EQUIPMENT

If you are a novice backpacker (and even if you are not), the question always is, "How little can I manage to take and still have everything I need?" This chapter should help you make some decisions about such items as backpacks, stoves, cooking equipment, and miscellaneous items.

BACKPACKS

There are many, many packs to choose from. One must consider such factors as the amount and kinds of gear taken, the terrain, and the duration of the trip. Packs can generally be divided into two categories: the soft pack and the external frame pack.

SOFT PACKS

Soft packs range from lightweight day packs to heavy-duty internal frame packs. Their uses vary from carrying books to school to long extended ski excursions.

Light Day Packs. These packs are usually used to carry light loads to school or to pack a picnic lunch to the mountains, or on other short excursions. Qualities to look for in selecting a day pack would be padded shoulder straps and good construction.

Heavy-duty Day Packs. These packs are usually a little heavier in construction and used for carrying heavier loads for longer periods of time. One should look for padded shoulder straps, good stitching, and a waist strap for improved balance.

Large Internal Frame Packs. Some activities require a large pack with narrow width and good balance. This type of pack can be used for ski touring, snowshoeing, winter mountaineering, and technical climbing. It will be warmer during hot weather than the external frame pack because the pack fits next to the back when in use. Qualities to look for in purchasing the pack are padded shoulder straps, good construction, and padded hip belt to help shift some of the weight from the shoulders.

External Framepack

Another choice for overnight and extended trips is a pack with a heavy-duty external frame and a sturdy, full-size bag (fig. 155). Such packs provide sturdy support and make heavy loads easier to carry. The frame should be of high quality tubular aluminum—sturdy, yet flexible enough to absorb shock. The frame is contoured to fit the body and is suspended by padded shoulder straps and a padded hip belt. Attached to the frame are two wide (often padded) strips of nylon mesh or cotton that allow the frame to rest comfortably against the back. The pack is in this way positioned close to the back but with enough separation for air to circulate between the frame and back, avoiding the sweaty, full-length contact of most soft packs. The design of the pack makes it possible for heavy loads to be carried in an upright position with most of the weight being supported by the hips.

Fig.155. Heavy-duty framework

A good pack allows adjustment of both frame and bag to provide the correct fit for each individual.

The bag should be of strong, tear-resistant nylon. It is often convenient to have a compartmentalized bag for easy packing, though some people prefer a single large compartment for maximum usable space. Outside pockets are helpful for frequently used equipment. High-quality bags are double- or triple-stitched with synthetic thread (cotton will rot in time). The bag should be attached to the frame with clevis pins and locking wire, or bolts and locking nuts, not with flimsy cord loops sewn to the bag. The bag should be easily removable. Some models allow the use of the bag with or without the frame.

Inspect the quality of materials and workmanship of the pack closely before you buy. Imagine yourself twenty miles back in the mountains with a broken pack, gear spilled all over the ground!

PACKING A BACKPACK

There are three important considerations in packing a backpack: (1) organizing equipment, (2) providing easy access to important articles of equipment, and (3) distributing the load for maximum comfort and efficiency.

Organization and Accessibility

Nylon ditty bags or plastic sacks are helpful in keeping gear organized and in providing extra protection from water that may leak through the pack bag. Bags also keep the gear compact, making it easier to pack (fig. 156).

Everyone eventually works out his own system of arranging his gear, but important items such as rain gear and some food and necessary clothing should obviously be within easy reach. In inclement weather, it is convenient to have the tent ready for unpacking first and repacking last.

Fig.156. Gear organized to be packed

Weight Distribution

The most important consideration in packing is centering the load over one's vertical walking axis, or center of gravity. The design of the pack helps greatly in centering the weight, but bad packing can keep any pack from riding correctly.

Avoid weighing down the lower portion of the pack. Too much weight too low will cause an unnatural pull on the back and will strain both the back and leg muscles. When the load is correctly centered, it will normally ride fairly high on the back.

The weight distribution will also vary according to what you are doing—hiking, skiing, or climbing. For most normal backpacking, the heavier objects are best placed nearer the top of the pack, with the lighter and bulkier items farther down.

Hoisting the Pack

Putting on a heavy pack is not as easy as it might seem (figs. 157 to 161). You should develop a system for hoisting a pack without help from another person or even a rock to balance it on.

Using your own knee or bent leg as a support will help. Swing the pack onto the leg and rest it there while you put one arm through the shoulder strap. Then lean forward and push with the bent leg, swinging the pack onto the back and putting the other arm and both shoulders through and into position in a continuous motion.

When the pack is seated on your shoulders, lean forward again, hunch your shoulders, and slide the pack up your back so that you can cinch the padded waist belt securely over your hips. When you stand straight, the weight should fall naturally onto your hips. Be sure the shoulder straps are tight enough to keep the pack in line and the weight close to your back.

LIGHTWEIGHT STOVES

The lightweight stove has become one of the backpacker's most important pieces of equipment. With the increasing numbers of enthusiasts taking to the outdoors, firewood has grown scarce in many areas, and natural beauty has suffered with the removal of timber and

Fig.157. Pack resting on knee

Fig.158. Putting arm through shoulder strap

Fig.159. Swinging the pack onto the back

Fig.160. Cinching waist belt over hips

144

Fig.161. Pack in line

picturesque snags. In many wilderness areas, campfires are prohibited, and much of the alpine terrain so popular with hikers is naturally limited in timber growth. What does survive the rigorous climates at high elevations is vital to the ecology and scenic value of the area. Open, meadow-covered areas are extremely fragile, and the black, charred remains of old fire pits are a blemish on the beauty of the wilderness.

There is a great variety of stoves on the market, and it can be a confusing task to select the one most suited to the kinds of trips you will be taking. Most of the lightweight stoves have one burner and weigh from 1 to 3 pounds. Consider such factors as: climatic conditions, terrain, duration of the trip, distance traveled, number of people in the party, availability of water, and the kinds of foods to be cooked. No stove will ideally meet all conditions, so be prepared to compromise.

Stoves are generally classified under the type of fuel used. The four most common fuels are: alcohol, kerosene, liquefied petroleum gas, and gasoline.

Alcohol Stoves

Alcohol stoves are the simplest, with no pumping or priming required. They are lightweight and inexpensive. Alcohol is one of the safest fuels; it will not explode or burn out of control.

Alcohol is not a very efficient fuel, however, for it has a low heat output and low burning rate. Its use is limited to stoves designed for light cooking and favorable conditions. A familiar example is the Sterno folding stove, consisting simply of a cup in which jellied alcohol is burned.

Kerosene Stoves

The kerosene stove requires both pumping and priming, but it is a relatively efficient fuel after it is burning. Kerosene is a reasonably safe, explosion-proof fuel, though it is somewhat messy, because of its oily nature and slow evaporation. Odorless grades are now available. Kerosene is a less expensive fuel. It is not commonly used in the United States, but it is often the only readily available fuel in many other countries.

Liquefied-Petroleum Gas Stoves

Two basic fuels come under this heading: propane and butane. Propane comes in relatively heavy containers because of the high pressure needed to liquefy the gas, and while it is an excellent fuel, it is more often used in car camping than in backpacking.

Butane stoves are popular with backpackers because of their simplicity and light weight (fig. 162). The gas comes in disposable cartridges attachable to the stove unit. The stoves do not require pumping or priming, and they provide an effective heat source that can be regulated from a full boil down to a fine simmer.

The effectiveness of some butane stoves decreases with cold temperatures and high winds. Under normal conditions, they are easy to light, but in extreme cold, the gas often lacks sufficient pressure to vaporize. Butane stoves are generally less expensive than gasoline stoves, but the cost of the fuel itself is much higher.

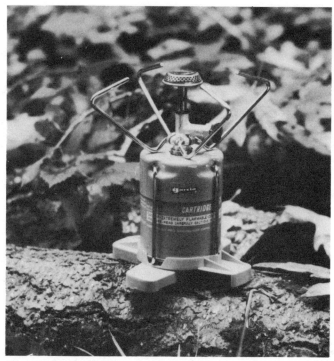

Fig.162 . Butane Stove

Gerry, Optimus, EFI, Bleue (Gaz) Primus, and Bluett are common brands of butane stoves.

Gasoline Stoves

The type of gasoline most commonly used in outdoor stoves is a highly refined form of white gas called stove or lantern fuel. Coleman fuel is a popular example. The many varieties of gas stoves range from small lightweight models to bigger, heavier versions designed for maximum heat output. All need to be primed, and some utilize a pump as well. Gas stoves are usually a bit heavier than butane stoves, but the models designed for backpacking fall well within the acceptable weight limit (fig. 163).

A separate stainless steel bottle of fuel must be carried for refilling the stove. Gas stoves offer an efficient heat source under many conditions, but they function best at high heat levels and are not as good as butane stoves for simmering.

Fig.163. Gas stove and cooking equipment

For winter camping, stoves with a pump are most successful, and some of the higher-powered gas stoves function well even in extremely cold temperatures.

Gas stoves are somewhat more expensive than butane stoves, but the fuel is cheaper. Some of the more popular gas stoves are made by Optimus, Phoebus, and M.S.R.

increasing the effectiveness of your stove. The performance of any stove can be greatly increased by intelligent operation. Wind and cold can drastically reduce the efficiency of any stove, and the successful backpacker knows how to control or minimize the effects of these two elements. Most stoves come with their own built-in or attachable wind protection devices, some more successful than others. Much can be done in selecting a sheltered place for operation, constructing additional windbreaks, and keeping fuel bottles, cartridges, and stoves out of the cold by wrapping them in clothing or storing them in sleeping bags overnight.

Safety and care of stoves. Intelligent use and care of your stove not only help prevent broken parts in the wilderness, but may also avert a serious accident.
- Take care not to overheat any stove, particularly one using butane or gasoline.
- In insulating the stove from wind and cold, be sure you don't cut off the oxygen supply to the stove or create an oven-like effect whereby the stove bakes in its own heat.
- Avoid operating the stove in a closely confined area, such as a tent, and do not pile dirt or rocks too closely around it.
- Keep the size of pots and pans small to avoid reflecting too much heat back onto the stove.
- Keep the stove and fuel containers away from other sources of heat.
- Butane is highly flammable and care must be taken when changing cartridges; be sure that all the gas is used up before removing the cartridge. Even then, some gas will escape.
- Gasoline stoves must be primed carefully. Avoid drenching the priming cup with too much fuel; only a small amount is needed.
- Know the construction and operation of your stove thoroughly, so that you can both prevent and identify malfunctions.
- Inspect and clean your stove frequently, replacing worn-out or damaged parts.

COOKING EQUIPMENT

Simplicity and multi-use are the key words in selecting cooking equipment. Take only what is needed, and then use your imagination to concoct a varied menu with limited equipment (fig. 164).

Fig.164. Basic cooking equipment

Pots and Pans

If your party is limited to two or three persons, often a 2- or 3-quart pot with a lid is sufficient. The lid can serve as a pan for frying or as an extra plate. For larger parties, choose a set of pots, pans, and plates of various sizes that nest together into one compact unit. Some pot-and-pan kits dispense with handles to save space; in this case, a potholder is a necessary implement.

All utensils should be either of stainless steel or of aluminum. A fine aluminum, lightweight, but thick enough for durability and even heat distribution, is a good choice. Avoid iron and other heavy metals.

In pots and pans you usually get what you pay for.

All-Purpose Cup

A stainless steel cup is an indispensable tool with many uses. It can be used for hot and cold liquids, cereals, soups, stews, puddings, etc. It can even serve as a pot in which to cook or as a plate for portions of a main course. The cup can also be a handy tool for measuring.

Be sure to buy a cup with a heat-resistant handle. If you want a deeper cup, there are several insulated unbreakable plastic cups on the market.

One of the most frequently used brands of stainless steel cups is the "Sierra" cup.

Water Bottle

Polyethylene bottles are the best choice, as they are lightweight and clear. Some types of polyethylene tend to absorb odors and bacteria. There should be no carry-over of taste or smell between fillings when the bottle is properly cleaned.

Choose a durable bottle; some are too flimsy for the rough use they will probably receive. Be sure that the bottle has a gasket in the lid; if not, you should install one to prevent leaks.

Metal containers are not good choices because they are heavy and can become very cold, freezing the contents and making them difficult to handle.

Utensils

You'll need a lightweight stainless steel knife-fork-spoon set that nests together. Also include a can opener and a good pocketknife.

Miscellaneous Items

Plastic or nylon "ditty" bags are excellent to compartmentalize food, small items, and cooking and eating equipment.

A spillproof combination salt and pepper shaker is useful.

All kinds of culinary gadgets can be purchased, many of which are convenient, but not really necessary. Some examples: plastic containers of all sizes and shapes, plastic egg carriers, nylon spatulas, squeeze tubes for liquids and spreadables, ladles, and fold-up grills.

SHELTER AND SLEEPING BAGS

SHELTER

The hiker's continual exposure to potentially severe weather conditions makes shelter a very important consideration in backpacking. The backpacker is on his own, away from civilization, roads, and facilities. If the weather turns bad, he must accept it and be prepared to cope with it; he cannot climb into his car and head for the warmth of his home or an inn. Careful selection must be made from a specialized line of equipment to insure an adequate shelter.

Capacity

The lightweight camper must make do with a minimum of room. His shelter will have much less space than a tent used for car camping with a corresponding number of people. Backpacking and "mountain" tents usually range from a one-person to a four-person capacity, the most popular being for two and three persons.

Some tents feature a second entrance, usually in the shape of a tunnel, which may be used for joining two tents together. Many tents feature a vestibule—an extension of the main body of the tent—in which gear can be stowed. If you will be spending a lot of time in the tent, or if you simply prefer more room, remember to choose a larger tent.

Weight and Bulk

Since the lightweight camper must carry his shelter on his back, concern tends to shift away from capacity toward ease of transport. Emphasis is on maximum protection and durability with a minimum of weight and bulk. One- to two-person tents usually range anywhere from 3 to 9 pounds. Three- and four-person tents weigh from 9 to 12 pounds.

Ease of Assembly

Backpackers need a tent that is simply put together, with a minimum of parts. Setting up camp often takes place in windy, cold, and wet weather. At such times the backpacker appreciates a tent that is pitched easily, with no complications or frustrating obstacles. Ease in setting up and breaking camp is also desirable; backpackers generally tend to move their camp frequently.

Materials and Construction

Most lightweight tents are made of tightly woven, rip-stop nylon. Cotton is not suitable, as it is relatively heavy and bulky. Nylon is not only light; it compacts well and is easily packed.

Look for a durable nylon with strong, well-stitched seams and high-quality workmanship. Mosquito netting should cover all entrances and ventilation holes.

The tent should also have a coated nylon rain-fly. The rain-fly (fig. 165) will help keep the inner tent dry in foul weather, and it will help reduce the condensation if it is properly fitted to the tent. Poles are usually made of aluminum or fiberglass and come in easily assembled, interlocking sections.

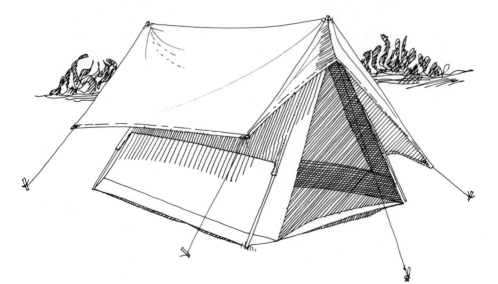

Fig.165. Rain fly

Types of Shelter

Tents. The most common lightweight-tent design is the A-frame (fig. 166). Many other designs have proved effective as well, such as the dome (fig. 167), the pyramid (fig. 168), and the cascade (fig. 169).

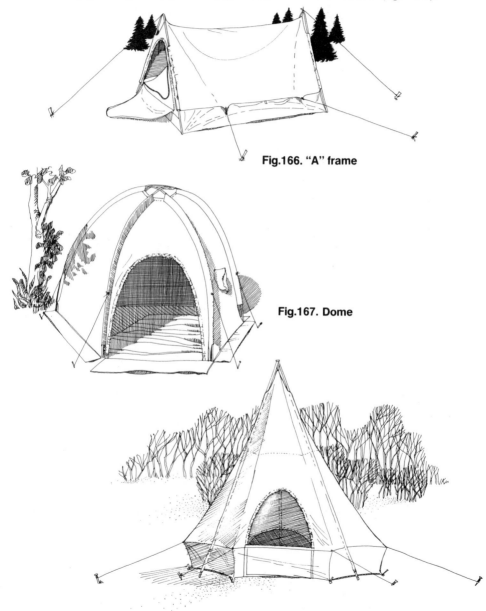

Fig.166. "A" frame

Fig.167. Dome

Fig.168. Pyramid

Fig.169. Cascade

Tube tents are simple continuous polyethylene tarps with open ends (fig. 170). Some come with grommets for cords, which are fastened to trees or poles for support and anchoring. Tube tents are inexpensive and very lightweight. However, they are not very durable or secure and suffice only in non-windy, dry conditions. Tube tents make a good emergency shelter.

Fig.170. Tube

Makeshift shelters. Three kinds of makeshift shelters are popular with backpackers.

- The tarp. If your concern is not so much durability and comfort as it is financial, and if you're traveling in good weather and want a quick, convenient shelter for the night, carry along a tarp (figs. 171 to 172). Always have enough rope to secure the tarp. Trees are often not in the right locations, so you might consider taking poles.
- The poncho. Not very large, the poncho can nevertheless double as a walking protection against the weather and a small tent, if you carry poles, pegs, and lines (fig. 173).
- The groundsheet. A large plastic grommeted groundsheet can act as a ground protection and an angled roof at the same time. Remember, though, that stones and sharp twigs will puncture it. Don't plan to keep it long. And don't leave it in the woods to create an unsightly mess (fig. 174).

Accessories

Groundsheet. It is a good idea to carry along a lightweight tarp to put under your tent. Tent floors on most backpacker tents are very lightweight and thin. The tarp will assist in keeping out moisture, and it will help protect the floor, adding life to the tent.

Stakes. Carry along stakes of lightweight aluminum, plastic, or fiberglass.

Care of Shelter

Waterproofing. Nylon tents will leak along the seams where holes have been made by the needle in stitching. It is a good idea to seal these areas before use. Sealant comes in paste, liquid, or spray.

Airing. Every tent should be kept dry whenever possible. Be sure your tent is well dried and aired before storing for more than a day or two. At home, store the tent in a dry, cool place out of the sun. Roll it up loosely in a box or bag. Sunlight (ultraviolet rays) tends to weaken nylon in time.

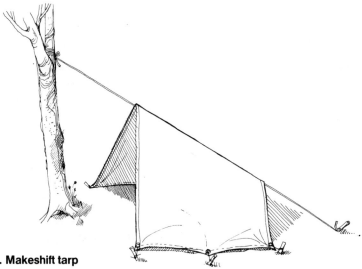

Fig.171. Makeshift tarp

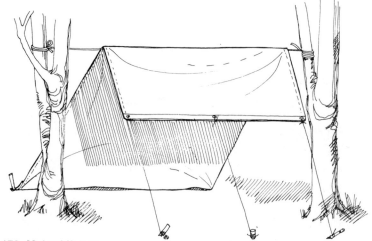

Fig.172. Makeshift tarp

 Fig.173. Poncho

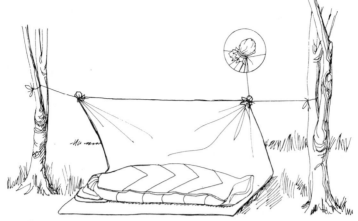

Fig.174. Groundsheet

Cleaning. Always keep your tent clean. Grit and dirt not only contribute to discomfort; they can seriously wear away at the delicate materials of your tent. Always clean your tent when your trip is over, shaking it out and wiping it or washing it by hand.

SLEEPING BAGS

Sleeping gear is very important if you are a backpacker, because you are exposed to extremes in weather. Weight is crucial; your bag must have maximum warmth with a minimum of bulk and weight. Choose a bag that will meet the requirements for your outing. Most sleeping bags are rated for warmth by the manufacturer, but these ratings are very general and may not apply in every case, because of the great variability in individual metabolism.

Sleeping Comfort

The purpose of your sleeping equipment is to protect you from the cold and to provide you with comfortable and relaxing sleep.

When you are camping out, approximately one-third of your time is spent sleeping. You will not be able to work or play to your full potential without a good night's rest. Because of this (and because of the cost of sleeping equipment), it is essential that you use care in selecting the kind of sleeping gear that will meet your needs.

No one sleeping bag is ideal for all purposes, so looking for a sleeping bag to fit your individual needs is important. Weather, body metabolism, clothing, ground insulation, shelter, and bag construction will all help determine the degree of warmth and the comfort of the bag.

Weather. Obviously, weather is an important consideration in your choice of a sleeping bag. At least three weather factors will affect your sleeping comfort.

■ Temperature. Your main concern with temperature when you are camping is usually how to stay warm at night rather than how to keep cool. Be sure you investigate the temperature of a place before you decide to camp there; then get a sleeping bag with sufficient insulation to cope with that temperature. A good rule of thumb is to remember that in 40° F. weather (without wind), you should have a bag with 3 to 5 inches of insulation. This means, of course, that the insulator is filling all the space in the bag. If a sleeping bag has 6 inches of loft (air space), you will probably have only 3 inches of insulation. Even 12 inches of loft in a down bag will compress to less than 1 inch of down. Remember this when you purchase your bag, and compress either the top or the bottom of the bag to discover its true thickness. Sometimes, however, the loft allows no air to circulate, and this dead air space will help to keep you warm.

■ Wind (moving air). Wind affects body temperature in two ways:
  1. Moving air sweeping across your sleeping bag will carry heat away.
  2. Moving air will diffuse through the material of your bag, lowering the temperature.

Thus, if your campsite is windy, take with you a bag with thicker insulation than the temperature calls for (or use shelter—or a windproof bag).

■ **Humidity.** Humidity is the degree of moisture in the atmosphere. Just as humidity in hot weather makes the heat more unbearable, humidity in cold weather increases the chill. Allow another 1 to 2 inches of insulation for a camping site with high humidity.

Body metabolism. Many things affect your body metabolism, and it must be considered when you are looking for a sleeping bag.

■ Physical condition. If you are "out of shape," tired, and hungry, you are more apt to become cold than if you are in tip-top shape. While most campers are disposed to be physically in tune, there are those who have fewer opportunities for camping and who find themselves to be very "soft" physically. If you are one of the latter, you may need a warmer bag than your physically fit counterpart.

- Intake of food before sleeping. Some foods, such as those containing sugar, increase your natural blood sugar and thus create heat in your body. If you eat such foods immediately before retiring, you will remain warmer than otherwise, especially if you eat them in great quantity. Hot drinks or hot food before retiring also help to warm the body.

Other factors, including emotional changes and changes in altitude, affect your body metabolism. Be prepared to compensate for these things by buying a sleeping bag that will keep you warm in spite of all of them.

Clothing. The kind and amount of clothing you wear inside your sleeping bag (too much tight clothing will make you cold) will contribute to your warmth and comfort.

- Dry clothing. Make sure you have a dry change of clothing to wear to bed. If you have been exerting yourself at hiking or working in the camp area, your clothing will probably be damp from perspiration. Remember that damp clothing will bring down the temperature inside your sleeping bag. Even if you haven't been exerting yourself and your clothes feel dry, moisture is present if you have been wearing them throughout the day. Be on the safe side; change your clothing before retiring.

- Loose clothing. Tight clothing, such as belts, ties, and elastic bands, cuts off badly needed circulation while you sleep. Make sure that no part of your body is constricted by such sleepwear. Get comfortable, loose clothing to wear in your sleeping bag. Stuff extra clothing around or underneath yourself if you are cold.

- Layers of clothing. Several layers of lightweight, loose clothing seem to keep out the chill better than one heavy layer. This is true, perhaps, because the air holes in one layer of material are backed by material in another.

Ground insulation. The down or fiber in your sleeping bag compresses under your weight and leaves very little thickness between you and the cold ground. Therefore, you need some kind of insulator to lay on the ground before you roll out your sleeping bag. A foam pad is better than an air mattress, since air circulates in an air mattress, causing it to remain cooler than the foam pad. And closed-cell foam pads are better insulators than open-cell foam pads, since closed cells do not allow air to circulate; they do not compress as easily; and they do not absorb moisture.

Shelter. Heat loss occurs more rapidly in the out-of-doors at night than under a lean-to, in a tent, or under some other form of cover. So, if you can stand to give up the pleasure of watching the stars overhead as you "sleep out" in cool weather, you will probably sleep more comfortably. Tents are available with netting to protect you from bugs, but you can still enjoy the splendor of the night. All good tents also come equipped with rain flaps for your protection.

Bag design and construction. The type of camping you want to do will help determine the kind of sleeping equipment you will use. For the backpacker, of utmost importance will be weight. There are two basic designs: The basic styles for sleeping bags are the mummy (fig. 175) and the rectangle (fig. 176). There are others, but they are usually modifications of these two.

    1. *The mummy bag* is rather lightweight and provides a minimum amount of dead air space. It is usually equipped with a hood that has drawstrings, and it tapers at the feet.

    2. *The rectangular bag* is heavier than the mummy, but provides for less restriction of movement.

Fig.175. Mummy bag

Fig.176. Rectangle bag

Cut of bag. The way a sleeping bag is cut can help prevent cold spots occurring in the bag. Here are two cuts for you to consider.

1. *Differential cut.* The differential cut in a sleeping bag is similar to the way a thermos bottle is put together. The inside of the bag is cut smaller so that when pressure is exerted against it, it doesn't touch the outside. This bag is warmer and lighter in weight than many others because its construction requires less material.

2. *Space filler.* The outside and the inside of the space-filler bag are cut the same size. When pressure is put on a point (when the inside of the bag touches the outside) such as an elbow pushing on the side of the bag, cold spots similar to the sewn-through construction types can be created. It is less expensive than the differential cut because it does not require as much labor on its construction.

Construction of sleeping bags. The internal design of a sleeping bag can affect the warmth of it. Following are a few basic types of construction for sleeping bags:

1. Sewn through: The least expensive, and also the most likely to have cold spots, especially at the seams. The tubes formed by the stitching are filled with fiber or down. Not good for sleeping in the cold, but satisfactory for summer camping (fig. 177).

2. Box: Parallel nylon tabs sewn together, helping to prevent the shifting of down. The square tubes may collapse, and it is possible for down to shift unevenly, creating cold spots (fig. 178).

3. Slant wall: Down from one compartment overlapping to down

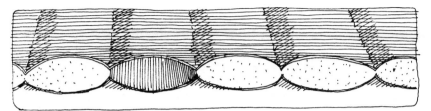

Fig.177. Sewn-through

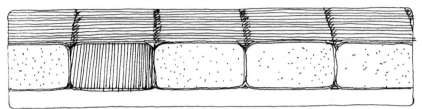

Fig.178. Box

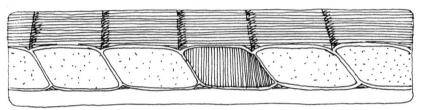

Fig.179. Slant wall

in another compartment, thus reducing down shift and cold spots more efficiently than the square box, though not as well as the V-tube (fig. 179).

4. V-tube: Overlapping triangular tubes somewhat restricting loft but also restricting down shift and cold spots very efficiently (fig. 180).

5. Laminated: Two layers of quilting sewn together. The seams of one layer (the thin part) lie against the thick part of the other layer, compensating for cold spots in the bag (fig. 181). This is not a lightweight construction.

Types of fill for sleeping bags. Since heat is not produced by the sleeping bag, the purpose of the fill is to retain the heat produced by the body. The fill (and the construction of the tube that holds the fill) will create dead air space (the loft) and comfort range. The loft, or the ballooning and puffing effect, refers to the thickness of the insulation. The thicker the loft, the warmer the bag. *Comfort zone* refers to the degree of temperature the bag is designed for. Because there are no

164

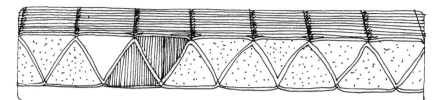

Fig.180. V-tube

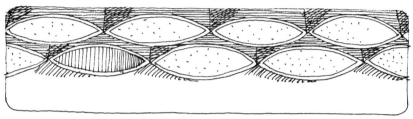

Fig.181. Laminated

set government regulations and no set body condition, the comfort zone will vary; but it may be used as a guide.

The following are the two basic fills for sleeping bags:

1. Down. Down comes from geese or ducks and may be either plain or sized. Goose down is often selected over duck, but they are similar in performance. Sized down, recently placed on the market, is heavier, but it takes less of it to create the same amount of warmth created by duck or goose down. The main disadvantage of down is that if it becomes wet, it is difficult to dry and will tend to lose most of its loft (and therefore its insulating capacity).

2. Fiber. Fiber fill is heavier and bulkier than down and not so fluffy. A fiber bag does not absorb water so easily; it will dry much faster than down and will retain its loft better when wet. It loses loft faster when it becomes older and breaks down more quickly than down.

Some sleeping bags on the market use down for the upper section and fiber for the lower one. Down-filled bags cost more than fiber-filled ones but generally last longer. Evaluate your needs and find the bag to meet them.

CAMPING KITS

You can make your own sleeping bag by purchasing a ready-to-make kit. The following is a list of what most manufacturers include in a backpacking kit. Instructions and materials....

- for sewing together backpacking clothing such as down- or foam-filled pants, jackets, parkas, shirts, and other items for use in cold weather.
- for making different kinds of sleeping bags, pads, and liners.
- for making backpacking tents or tube tents and ponchos.
- for making miscellaneous items to keep you warm, from foot warmers and mittens to down quilts.

Reasons for Making a Kit

When you set out to make something for yourself, usually, you don't do it just to fill time. That "something" you decide to make is often a top priority item that was put high on your list for very good reasons. If any of the following motives for making your own equipment inspire you, you might get "hooked" into being a do-it-yourself backpacker.
- If you are interested in saving money, a kit can help you do that. Depending upon the items you decide to make, you can save from one-third to over one-half the price of the ready-made articles. Remember, though, you trade off savings in money for expenditure in time.
- Your home-sewn articles can be superior to ready-made ones because you can take the time to reinforce seams and to add extras like sectioned pockets and longer-length jackets for more warmth; you can make your sleeping bags longer, shorter, wider, or narrower, fuller, or flatter. On the other hand, the finished product may not be as good if the construction is poor.
- When you have made something for yourself, you tend to appreciate it more than when you buy a ready-made item. You know the care and time that have gone into putting it together, and you have that pride of ownership that motivates you to take better care of your possession.

The number of manufacturers putting out backpacking kits is increasing annually. More and more people are becoming self-sufficient in as many ways as possible, and factories are working hard to provide them with the materials to satisfy their desire to make-it-themselves. For backpacking kits, go to any well-established retail backpacker store. If they haven't any kits, they can probably suggest a manufacturer.

FOOD

Being creative in planning and cooking lightweight meals out-of-doors can be wonderfully rewarding—or it can be frustrating and expensive if you don't have the know-how.

For excellent eating on the trail, I recommend using a combination of supermarket foods, some fresh foods that travel well (depending on the length and the weight allowance of the trip), and home-dried foods (covered in chapter 10).

TRIPPING TIPS

If you give the necessary time and thought to the food you will take with you on your hiking trip, you will enjoy it more. Here are some tips to help you.

Meal Planning

Well-planned, nutritious meals are a must for the backpacker, not only to keep energy levels high, but also to keep spirits high. Good food is always a principal ingredient of good times.

The "basic four" foods. The basics of good meal planning apply on the trail as well as in the kitchen. Try to plan your meals around the "basic four" food groups, including the following: four or more servings daily of fruits and vegetables, four or more of breads and cereals, two servings of dairy products, and two servings from the meat group (may include other good protein sources such as legumes and nuts).

Bulk and weight. Since bulk and weight are important considerations in lightweight camping, take foods that will have the highest caloric and nutritional value for their respective weight and bulk. Foods high in carbohydrates and fats are proportionately higher in calories.

General meal planning suggestions. Plan simple breakfasts consisting mainly of nutritious trail foods with a hot cereal or drink on cold mornings, lunches that can be eaten along the way, and dinners with one hot dish.

In planning daily menus, remember these basic principles:
Variety (a steady diet of anything gets old pretty fast)
Flavor (some foods spicy, some bland)
Texture (crunchy, soft, chewy)
Temperature (hot, cold)
Color (food that looks good somehow always tastes better)

Packaging

Food should be premeasured and repacked in small plastic bags for daily use. Depending on the length of the trip and individual preference, compartmentalize the food accordingly: "trail food," "breakfasts," "dinners," or "foods to be cooked."

Reduce bulk wherever possible: squeeze excess air out of plastic bags, throw away any extra cardboard, foil wrappers, and any other extraneous materials.

Carefully package spillables and liquids in airtight plastic containers.

On the Trail

Reconstituting dehydrated foods. Add water to dehydrated vegetables during a lunch break (fig. 182). Remove the air and seal the bag. For added protection, place it in another bag and seal the second one also. Carry it on your pack as you hike toward your next campsite. The food will be reconstituted when you arrive. Home-dried foods usually take longer to reconstitute than freeze-dried foods.

Drinking water. Keep a folded plastic bag in your pocket. When you find a source of drinking water, fill the bag and drink from it (fig. 183).

Fig.182. Adding water to dehydrated vegetables

Fig.183. Drinking from plastic bag

169

When the bag is empty, keep it zipped so that the inside does not get dirty. Fold it and place it in your pocket again for the next use.

Mixing food. Mix foods such as cake mixes, pancake mix, meat loaf, and others in Zip-Lock or heavy plastic bags (fig. 184). Place the item to be mixed in the plastic bag on a flat surface, and with a hand on each side of the bag, move the hands to the top to force excess air out. Zip

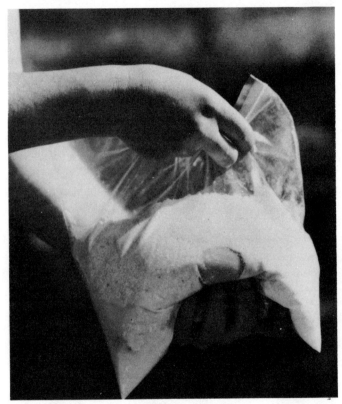

Fig.184. Mixing food in Zip-Lock plastic bag

the bag shut, and holding the bag in one hand, squeeze the food with the other. Each squeeze is equal to one stir. (Caution: long fingernails can puncture the plastic bag.)

Setting Jell-O. Following the directions on the package, dissolve the Jell-O in water. Place the mixture in a Zip-Lock bag and remove as much air as possible. Seal it and place it in a cool place, such as in a stream. To form the Jell-O, place the bag inside a # 10 can.

170

No-Cook Recipes

Here are three "goodies" you might make without lighting a fire.

No-Bake Chocolate Cake (Fig.185)

- Mix batter as directed on package of 1 chocolate cake mix
- Add   nuts, marshmallows, and coconut

If you like thick cake batter, add less liquid than package requires. This special treat served in an ice-cream cone (fig. 186).

Walking Salad

- Cut around the top of and remove core and seeds from   1 apple
- Add   raisins and 1 to 2 tablespoons chunky peanut butter
- Fill cavity in apple with the mixture (fig. 187).

This is a refreshing snack and provides quick energy on hikes. You might want to put the apple in a plastic bag to eat a snack on the trail.

**Fig.185. No-bake chocolate cake—
adding nuts and marshmallows**

Fig.186. No-bake chocolate cake in ice cream cone

Fig.187. Walking salad

172

Orange-with-Peppermint-Straw Drink

- Roll around on a hard surface and squeeze to loosen juice of   1 orange
- With a pocketknife or other slim, sharp blade, cut out one end of the orange, leaving a small hole (⅜'' in diameter). Slide the knife blade down into the hole and cut the meat in several places to release the juice (fig. 188). Into the hole insert one end of   1 peppermint stick (or porous candy) (fig. 189)

    Suck on the other end of the peppermint stick as you would a straw. The orange juice will come up through the peppermint stick. You might have to squeeze the orange periodically to loosen the juice.

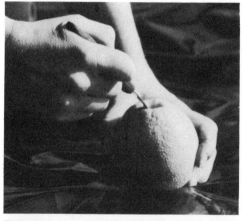

Fig.188. Cutting meat of orange

Fig.189. Peppermint stick for juice

173

Fig. 190. Supermarket foods

SUPERMARKET CONVENIENCE FOODS

You'll be amazed at the vast number of dried convenience foods available at supermarkets (fig. 190). Quality, price, and brand vary from store to store, but by checking the ingredients, weight, and price, you can make comparisons to get the most for your money.

Store brands are generally 5 to 20 percent less expensive than name brands and often as good in quality. Buying larger quantities, generally is less expensive.

Check to see what items need to be added to mixes (such as hamburger or eggs) before buying to make sure they are practical for your trip.

Supermarket mixes such as pancake or biscuit mix are usually about half as expensive as the ones found in backpacking supply stores. However, you can again cut the price in half by making your own.

I've divided the list of supermarket foods into:

Trail foods

Staples

174

Breakfast foods
Soups and stews
Meats and other proteins
Main dishes
Side dishes
Desserts
Beverages

Trail Foods

These are foods to eat on the trail when you don't want to bother with building a fire or lighting your stove, or when you just need an energy lift. They can be used to supplement meals.

Dried fruits
Apples (with variations—cinnamon, strawberry, etc.)
Apricots
Banana chips
Blueberries
Dates
Figs
Fruit rolls and fruit leather
Fruit-and-nut combinations
Peaches
Pears
Pineapple
Prunes
Raisins

Protein foods
Cheese
    hard
    squeeze-package cheese snacks
Fish, canned
Instant breakfast
Jerky
Meats, canned
Meat sticks
Nuts
Peanut butter

Breads and cereals
Bread sticks
Cookies (bar type), such as fig bars
Crackers that don't crumble easily
    Roman Meal Crackers
    Ry-Krisp
    Triscuits
Granola
Granola bars
Melba toast
Pop tarts

Candies (anything that doesn't melt or mash easily)
Hard candies
Gumdrops
Jelly beans

Staples
Flour
Honey
Instant milk
Jam
Margarine
Peanut butter
Salt and pepper
Spices
Sugar
    brown (brown sugar + water = syrup)
    granulated
Vegetable oil

Breakfast Foods
Bacon Bits
Bacon, canned, sliced
Bisquick
Breads, quick, compact—already baked
Breakfast squares, fortified
Cereals, hot, instant non-cooked
Cornbread mix
Dried fruits

French toast mix
Granola
Granola bars
Hash browns, dried
Meat sticks
Muffin and scone mixes
Pancake mix, complete
Pop tarts

Soups and Stews
Chili seasoning mix
Noodles, "Instant Oriental" and base
Soup, instant, powdered—just add hot water
Soup mixes, packaged, powdered—all varieties
Stew base mixes including
     Bouillon—instant or cubes
     Gravy mixes
     Powdered stock base mixes

Meats and Other Proteins
Bacon bits
Bacon, canned, sliced
     Chipped beef
     Deviled ham
     Lunchmeat
     Spam
     Vienna sausage
Cheese snacks (squeeze package)
Fish, beef, or chicken (canned)
Jerky
Meat sticks
Salami (dry)
Vegetable protein, texturized (available in chunk or granule form)
     Beef
     Chicken
     Ham
     Plain

Main Dishes (must add dehydrated hamburger or T.V.P. [Textured Vegetable Protein])

Hamburger Helper type
  Beef noodle
  Cheeseburger noodle
  Chili-tomato
  Hamburger stew
  Lasagne
  Potato Stroganoff
  Rice Oriental
  Spaghetti
Tuna Helper type (may add tuna, ham, chicken, or turkey chunks)
  Creamy noodles with vegetables
  Creamy rice
  Newburg
  Noodles and cheese sauce

Side Dishes (some of which may be adapted to main-course dinners)
Gravy mixes
Macaroni and cheese
Macaroni salad mixes
Mushrooms, sliced, dehydrated
Noodle mixes
Potatoes, dehydrated
  Flakes
  Powdered
  Shredded
  Sliced
Potato mixes
  Au gratin
  Scalloped
Rice, instant, pre-cooked
Rice mixes (Rice-a-Roni types)
Sauce mixes (sour cream, white sauce, teriyaki, sweet 'n' sour)
Tuna salad mixes
Vegetable flakes

Desserts
Cake mixes requiring only water
Cheesecake, instant
Danish dessert mix

Fruit cobblers
Fruit dumplings
Jell-O
Popcorn
Pudding, instant
Pudding snacks, canned (bulky but easy)

Beverages
Breakfast drinks, powdered, fruit-flavored
 Grape
 Grapefruit
 Orange
 Tomato
Cocoa mix, hot
Drinks (Kool-Aid type), powdered, fruit-flavored
 Artificially sweetened
 Presweetened with sugar
Milk, instant, dry
Milk flavorings
 Chocolate
 Strawberry

FRESH FOODS THAT TRAVEL WELL

If space and weight allow, you can take a number of fresh foods that will keep well without refrigeration for four or five days. Often you can use the fresh foods on the first couple of days of the trip, which means a lighter pack for the rest of the time. The following suggestions should help you to keep the food in top condition:
- Pack only fresh, unbruised, top-quality fruits and vegetables.
- Do not wash them before packing; it will cause the fruits and vegetables to deteriorate more quickly.
- For better insulation, pack foods that should be kept cooler in the center.
- Pack foods that crush or bruise more easily in side pockets or in cooking pots.
- Pack each fruit or vegetable in a brown paper bag that allows moisture to evaporate and retains freshness longer.

- When carrying fresh meats (usually for use on the first day), freeze solid, slit the plastic store wrapper, wrap in newspapers to insulate, and place the whole in a brown paper bag.

Fruits	**Vegetables**	**Breads**
apples	beans	breadsticks
citrus fruits	broccoli	dense whole-grain breads
melons	carrots	English muffins
	celery	hard-crust French and
	chili peppers	sourdough breads
	cucumbers	Middle East bread
	garlic	pumpernickel
	green peppers	rye
	mushrooms	tortillas
	onions	
	parsnips	
	peas	
	potatoes	
	spinach	
	sprouts	
	turnips	
	zucchini	

DRYING YOUR OWN FOODS

In considering dehydrated foods for camping, you have the option of buying the expensive prepackaged dehydrated or freeze-dried foods prepared especially for lightweight camping or preparing your own with the use of a home food dryer, your imagination, and your nearby supermarket.

Since the freeze-dried, prepackaged meals need no special preparation, I won't deal with them except to say that they are generally three to six times more expensive than comparable supermarket or home-dried items and frequently not as tasty. The only exception to this is meat—hamburger, in particular. You may choose to buy freeze-dried meats or hamburger to add to supermarket main-dish mixes.

DRYING YOUR OWN

Drying foods at home is becoming more and more popular as a means of preservation for general home use as well as for lightweight camping (fig. 191).

There are many advantages to drying your own foods. First of all, they occupy from only one-fifth to one-twentieth of the storage space and weight of canned or frozen foods. When properly stored, home-dried foods keep for at least a year, retaining top quality and nutritional value. Moreover, there is no danger of botulism with dehydrated foods. And you don't pay money to store them (as in your freezer); they may be stored simply in plastic bags inside moisture-proof metal or plastic containers. As with other methods of preservation, drying in season is a tremendous money-saver, adding interesting variety to home food stores and snacks.

Foods dried at home in your oven, or your dryer, or by the sun are all dried gradually. The moisture slowly evaporates because of an elevated temperature, and good air circulation removes the moisture.

These are some of the important factors covered here on home

Fig.191. Drying food at home

drying: methods of drying (sun, oven, and dehydrator); drying fruits and making fruit leather; drying vegetables; making jerky and other dried meats.

Methods of Drying

Methods of drying are almost as varied as the foods available to dry. For thousands of years, men used the sun to preserve food for use during the long winters. If you're lucky enough to live in a climate with long, hot summers and low humidity, you still may choose to sun-dry. However, if the weather isn't consistent where you live, you might want to try another method.

All you need is an increase in temperature to evaporate the moisture from the food fairly quickly and a good source of air to remove the moisture as it evaporates.

182

Beware of using a ventilation system from a furnace, because particles of dust, soot, or oil will settle on the food as it dries. Warm, relatively dust-free attics or basements may work fine for some foods. You might want to consider oven drying or a makeshift dryer.

However, if you plan to dry foods in any quantity, a dehydrator designed for that purpose is a must. You'll also find that food dried efficiently and at constant temperatures will have better color, flavor, and nutritional value.

The following pages will deal in greater detail with the different methods of drying.

Sun-drying. If you live in the Southwest, in or near the tropics, or wherever else you can count on five or more days of continuous sunshine, low humidity, and temperatures about 90°F. daily, you might want to try nature's way of preserving foods. Sun-drying is the oldest method of food preservation, and, depending on the locale, may be the easiest and least expensive.

Simply place food to be dried on screens (nylon-coated fiberglass) and find the warmest, sunniest, and safest spot in your yard. (By safest, I mean a place where the neighborhood dog, cat, or friend won't nibble up your goodies before they get dry.) Place the food as far away from dust, roads, and exhaust as possible. To protect it from birds and insects, cover it with cheesecloth or nylon netting—propped up so that it does not touch the food.

Be sure that the location has good air circulation, and if you choose to stack the screens after the food has partially dried, be sure to rotate them from top to bottom two or three times each day. Occasionally turning the fruit facilitates even drying. Stacking the screens during the last half of the drying process produces a nicer flavor and color because the food is less exposed to direct sunlight.

The food should be brought in at night or at the first sign of rain, because moisture on partially dried food will cause it to mildew and spoil.

Oven drying. If the weather in your area refuses to cooperate, oven drying may be a wise choice for home-drying foods. Since ovens vary in their range of temperature, size, and efficiency, experiment with yours to see what produces the best results.

Make a pillowcase-type covering out of nylon net to fit snugly over each oven rack so that the food can be dried on the net without falling through. If you want to dry larger quantities, try obtaining a couple of extra oven racks (frequently available from used appliance dealers) to make the most of your energy and the oven's. An average oven rack has about 2½ square feet; so with four racks, the total drying area would be about 10 square feet.

Load the racks with the food to be dried, leaving space between the foods for adequate air circulation. Do not overload the trays; this tends to result in unevenly dried food and longer drying times.

Set your oven to the lowest setting (ideally between 125° and 140°F.) and crack the oven door about ½ to 1 inch in an electric oven or 8 inches in a gas oven by inserting a pot holder or a lid near the door hinge. Check the oven temperature on each rack with an oven thermometer and adjust accordingly. In some gas ovens, the pilot light keeps the temperature warm enough. If your gas oven does not have an automatic shutoff valve, check it occasionally to make sure the flame is still on.

Rotate the racks every 2 to 3 hours for the most even drying. Cool the foods before you check them for dryness.

Homebuilt wood dryer. There are several limiting factors if you choose to build your own wood dryer. The first is safety. I cannot recommend using a wood dryer inside the home or the garage because of the possible fire hazard. With continued use, the wood continues to become drier until it may eventually reach a point where spontaneous combustion may occur, even at the relatively low temperatures used for drying. Wood dryers also tend to warp as they absorb the moisture from the drying foods. Wood has a tendency to absorb odors and may transfer flavors from one food to another. (Ever eat onion-flavored peaches?)

If you choose to make your own, consider the factors included in the section on buying a food dryer and make the necessary adaptations in whatever plan you decide to use.

Various plans for building your own dryer out of wood are available from the county extension service or state land grant university in most of the Western states. Check in your local county, and if they are not available, write to the State Extension Service in Utah, Idaho, Oregon, Washington, or California.

Dehydrators or commercial dryers designed for home use. A wide variety of commercial dryers are available, and you want to be sure to

184

get the safest, most efficient dryer for your money. Consider the following necessary components:

1. Heat source: This should be a consistent source of heat that can be thermostatically regulated. Heating cones are more efficient and react more rapidly to thermostatic control than do lightbulbs or nichrome wire.

- Air circulation: You will need a blower designed for continuous operation to circulate the air effectively. Squirrel-cage blowers are more efficient than fans.
- Thermostatic control: An accurate thermostat is necessary to maintain an even drying temperature. The variance in temperature should not exceed 3° to 5°. Water heater thermostats are not recommended because they frequently have a 15° to 20° variance. Food dried at a low, even temperature will have higher quality and greater nutritional value.

2. Safety features for this kind of dryer include the following:

- U.S. approval
- Nonflammable construction
- Enclosed electrical components
- Safety switch in case of thermostat failure
- Nontoxic screening (preferably nylon-coated fiberglass)
- Nontoxic paint

3. Initial cost: In order to get the most dryer for your money, compare the cost per square foot of drying area:

Cost ÷ sq. feet of drying area = cost per square foot

4. Cost of operation: The cost of operation depends on the wattage of the heating element. If a portion of the air recirculates within the dryer and the heating element is thermostatically controlled, the cost of operation will be lower. (The heating element does not have to run continuously.) The length of time the heating element runs depends on the following factors: recirculation of air, accuracy of thermostat, insulation in walls of dryer, dryer load, food moisture, and the external air temperature and humidity.

$$\frac{\text{watts} \times \text{time in hours (1)}}{1000} = \text{kilowatt hours}$$

kilowatt hours × kilowatt hour residential rate =
cost of operation per hour

(The kilowatt hour residential rate is available from the home service director of your utility company.)

5. Efficiency

Tray rotation: How much time is spent in tray rotation? The design of the dryer will determine this. Some dryers need not be rotated at all; others may require tray rotation every 2 to 3 hours.

Check the source of air flow. If it all comes from one source, trays will have to be rotated more frequently. If the air flow is diffused throughout the dryer (air vents near each tray), the food will dry more evenly.

Ease of loading: Are trays and food easily accessible?

Recirculating air: If the air is recirculated, it slightly reduces drying time.

6. Guarantee: Check for the location of the closest dealer and service. Also check for such things as length of guarantee, the shipping costs if the dryer needs to be returned to the manufacturer for repairs, what the guarantee covers, and how easily parts can be replaced after the warranty has expired.

Drying Fruits

Dried fruits are an ideal source of concentrated quick energy— usually eaten as they are. However, they can be rehydrated and used in pies, cakes, puddings, or even in fruit salads. Dried fruits weigh anywhere from one-fourth to one-twentieth of their fresh state. They may be stored and carried conveniently and are a delicious snack.

Only fresh, ripe fruits should be dried. Discard any bruised or overripe fruit. Allow underripe fruit to ripen slowly. Wash and handle the fruit carefully. Soaking prepared fruit in ascorbic acid solutions prevents excessive browning and increases the vitamin C content in dried fruit (figs. 192 to 194).

Fruits to be dried may be categorized in three groups:

Slice and dry (bananas, pineapple, etc.). Slice most fruits ¼″ to ⅜″ thick. Slice evenly where possible (rounds with even thickness dry more evenly than do wedges).

Fruits with edible skins (cherries, prunes, grapes. Most fruits with skins dry more quickly if the skins are broken by halving, pitting, or dipping in boiling water until the skins crack. Place on trays with skin side down to prevent dripping.

Fig.192. Preparing an apple

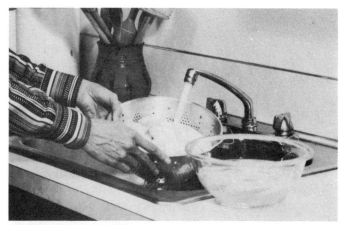

Fig.193. Rinsing apples

Fig.194. Sprinkling with jello

187

Fruits that oxidize (apples, pears, peaches, apricots). Fruits that oxidize contain enzymes that cause them to darken when they are cut and exposed to the air. They also lose their flavor and vitamins A and C during drying and storage if they are not pretreated by one of the methods listed below (in order of preference).

Pretreatment

1. Sulfuring (must be done outdoors with good ventilation): Sulfuring is the best method for preventing oxidation. The sulfur dioxide gas "seals" the surface area of the fruit, reducing loss of color, flavor, and vitamins A and C. During the drying process, the sulfur dioxide oxidizes, leaving no harmful chemicals on the fruit.

- Prepare the fruit. Hold in ascorbic-acid solution (1 teaspoon per ½ gallon water).
- Place fruit on trays (wood, nylon, or fiberglass) and stack trays 2" apart, using wooden blocks or spools on the corners.
- Place flowers of sulfur (sublimed sulfur) in clean shallow pan in front of trays of fruit. (Use 1 teaspoon sulfur per 2 pounds prepared fruit.)
- Cover stacked trays with a large cardboard box with 4 x 4-inch flaps cut in lower front and top back.
  Pack lower edges of the box with sand.
- Open flaps and ignite sulfur. Burn until almost consumed; close flaps.
- Let fruit set in sulfur box 30 minutes to 1 hour for thin slices, 1 to 1½ hours for halved fruit.
- Immediately place in dryer. Dryer should be in well-ventilated area outside for the first several hours of drying the sulfured fruit.

2. Sodium bisulfite, sodium sulfite, or potassium metabisulfite: Soaking fruit in one of these three solutions produces results similar to sulfuring in apples, peaches, and pears. These compounds are available from winemaking supply stores or drugstores. The procedure is as follows:

- Hold fruit in ascorbic acid solution (1 teaspoon per ½ gallon water).
- Soak fruit for 5 to 10 minutes in a solution of sodium bisulfite (1 tablespoon per gallon of water).
- Rinse. Place immediately in dryer.

3. Syrup blanching: If you prefer not using a sulfur method, syrup blanching may be used to produce a "candied" kind of dried fruit.

- Simmer prepared fruit 10 minutes in a solution containing 1 cup white corn syrup, 1½ cups sugar, and 3 cups water.
- Remove, drain, and place in dryer.

Conditioning

- After drying all fruits, place in closed container for one week (Tupperware, #10 can) to allow moisture to distribute equally.
- If there are any signs of condensation within the container, dry further.

Pasteurization

- Loosely place fruit in shallow pan and place in oven preheated to 175°F. Leave 15 minutes. Or place in dryer for 30 minutes at 160°F. This will kill any microorganisms not killed during the drying process.
- Cool.

Storage

- Package in Zip-Lock bags inside plastic containers (fig. 195).
- Store in dry, cool, dark place.

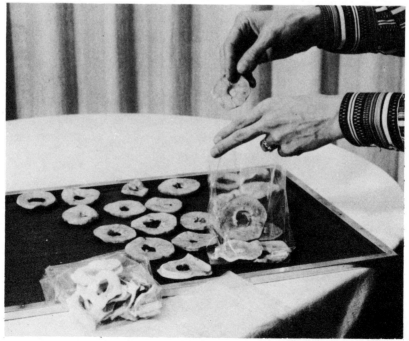

Fig.195. Packing dried apples

189

Fruit leather. Another fruit goody that is a favorite among lightweight campers is fruit leather, a chewy fruit roll made by pulverizing fresh fruit in the blender and drying it to a leatherlike consistency. Instructions for specific fruit leather are included in the chart on fruits, but you'll find some general information below that may be helpful.

- Use a teflon-coated cookie sheet or line-dryer trays with a plastic wrap designed for food use.
- Tape down the sides of the plastic wrap with masking tape to prevent the edges from lifting up during drying. (Waxed paper and foil should not be used in making leather because the fruit purée sticks.)
- Purée the fresh fruit in the blender until it is a smooth, even consistency.

Most fruits are delicious just as they are, but if the puréed fresh fruit isn't sweet enough for your taste, try sweetening it with honey or white corn syrup. (These help the leather maintain the chewy, leatherlike texture; granulated sugar tends to crystallize and make more brittle leather; brown sugar is somewhere in between.) Remember that the purée will concentrate in sweetness as it dries. Artificial sweeteners may also be used.

A small amount of lemon juice or ascorbic acid added to the purée tends to bring out the natural fruit flavor, and it increases the vitamin C content of the fruit leather.

- Spread the purée over the plastic wrap or cookie sheet until it is about ¼-inch thick, leaving at least 1-inch free around the edges (fig. 196). Dry it until it is pliable but not sticky to the touch. Peel off and roll like a jelly roll.

Fig.196. Pouring puree

Fig.197. Cutting leather in rolls

■ Cut the leather roll in 4-inch pieces, wrap each piece individually in plastic wrap (fig. 197), and label. (Many fruit leathers look alike.) Place the wrapped rolls in a moisture-proof container or Zip-Lock bag for storage. Do not refrigerate. Store in a cool, dark place.

Variations

1. *Canned fruit*

    Canned fruit makes delicious leather. Simply drain the syrup and purée the fruit in the blender. Many fruits combine nicely with fresh pineapple for a fresher flavor. Use one part fresh pineapple purée to three parts canned fruit purée.

2. *Leather pinwheels*

    Try spreading a filling (see date filling under chart on fruit) over the dried leather, rolling it and cutting it into pieces.

3. *Leather combinations*

    Try rolling two or three different fruit leathers together and cutting them into pieces.

4. *"Crunchy" leathers*

    Sprinkle chopped nuts, coconut, or granola over fruit leather and roll it. If it is kept longer than two weeks, store it in a freezer.

191

FRUIT	PREPARATION FOR DRYING	DRYNESS TEST	SPECIAL FRUIT LEATHER INSTRUCTIONS	BACKPACKING SUGGESTIONS
SLICE AND DRY				
Bananas	Slice 1/4". Riper bananas will turn darker and have a stronger flavor.	Leathery to crisp	Combines nicely with orange and pineapple; or sprinkle with nuts.	Try dipping in dry Jell-O. Dip in honey / lemon juice mixture and then in sesame seeds or chopped nuts.
Coconut	Crack shell; drain milk and steam 30 seconds to loosen from shell; peel, grate, and dry.	Leathery	May be sprinkled on fruit leathers as a garnish, but leather must then be stored in the freezer.	To sweeten: shake coconut in powdered sugar prior to drying. Use in fruit balls and granola.
Oranges	Slice in 1/4" rings with peel.	Crisp	Only in combination with other fruits.	Eat peel and all.
Pineapple	Pare, core, and slice in 3/8" rings.	Leathery	Combines well with apricot or canned fruit to add fresh flavor.	Good in trail mix or gorp.
Rhubarb	Wash, slice in 1" pieces and steam until tender.	Crisp	Combine with strawberry purée and sweeten with Karo or honey.	Best in fruit leather.

Fruit	Preparation	Dryness	Special Instructions	Uses
Strawberries	Wash, remove stems, slice 3/8" or halve and dip in ascorbic acid solution (1 tsp. per cup water).	Leathery to crisp	Purée; sieve through tea strainer.	Sprinkle with strawberry Jell-O for a "candied" strawberry.

FRUITS WITH EDIBLE SKINS

Fruit	Preparation	Dryness	Special Instructions	Uses
Berries	Raspberries, boysenberries, and blackberries are best in leathers. Too seedy to dry alone.		Purée and sieve to remove part of seeds. Add 2 tsp. powdered pectin per qt. of purée. Warm to bath temp., or mix with apple purée for leather without added pectin.	Leather is good in fruit balls or trail mix.
Blueberries	Wash and dry.	Leathery	Too bland. Use in combination with other fruits. One part each of blueberry, huckleberry, raspberry, and apple is delicious.	Eat like raisins or rehydrate for use in pancakes or muffins.
Cherries	Wash, pit, or halve.	Leathery	Warm purée until hot throughout; add ½ tsp. almond extract per 2 cups purée. Combine with	Eat like raisins or in trail mix.

FRUIT	PREPARATION FOR DRYING	DRYNESS TEST	SPECIAL FRUIT LEATHER INSTRUCTIONS	BACKPACKING SUGGESTIONS
			raspberry, apples, or pineapple.	
Dates	Pit, slice lengthwise, or cube in ½" cubes. May be rolled in lemon juice and then in granulated or brown sugar, then dried.	Leathery to very firm	May be used as a natural sweetening in other fruit leathers.	Use date filling to "sandwich" together two sheets of apricot leather. Date filling: cook 8 oz. dates, ½ cup sugar, ½ cup water, and 1 tsp. lemon juice until thickened.
Grapes	Wash, halve, or leave whole. May be dipped in boiling water to crack skins.	Leathery	Concord grapes: steam, sieve seeds, purée. Sweeten with honey or white Karo. Combines nicely with apple	To make raisins: use Thompson's seedless grapes.
Plums and Prunes	Wash, halve, and quarter. Remove pits. Dry skin side down. May be sulfured.	Leathery	Wash, pit, and purée. If very runny, add 2 tsp. pectin and warm. Combines nicely with apple.	Sprinkle with Jell-O for different flavor. Good in trail mix.

FRUITS THAT OXIDIZE

Apples	Pare, core, and slice in ¼" rings. Crisp, tart varieties dry best. Sulfur or soak in sulfite solution.	Leathery to crisp	Pare, core, cook until soft; purée. May add cinnamon, nutmeg, or red cinnamon candies. May use canned applesauce. Just purée.	Chop dry apples in blender to make "instant" applesauce mix. Sprinkle apple slices with Jell-O or cinnamon-sugar mixture just before drying.
Apricots	Wash, halve, and remove pits. Sulfur treatment preferred. Or syrup blanch, if you'd rather.	Leathery	Pit, purée, and warm to bath temperature. Combines well with pineapple; or honey or brown sugar may be added.	Sprinkle halves with Jell-O prior to drying.
Peaches or Nectarines	Wash, blanch, cool, peel, and remove pits. Slice ½" crosswise. Sulfur or soak in sulfite solution.	Leathery	Purée and warm; sweeten with honey if desired. Combines nicely with fresh pineapple (1 part pineapple purée to 3 parts peach).	Good in trail mix.
Pears	Wash, pare, core, and slice in rings or lengthwise in ½" slices. Sulfur or soak in sulfite solution.	Leathery	Purée and warm. Combines nicely with apple. May be flavored with red cinnamon candies.	Good in trail mix. Sprinkle with flavored Jell-O.

195

Drying Vegetables

Most vegetables dry well and retain the greater part of their nutrients, color, and flavor. Vegetables are scarce among commercially dehydrated foods and supermarket convenience foods. It is definitely an advantage to dry your own.

PREPARATION

With a few exceptions, vegetables need to be blanched prior to drying to inactivate enzymes which cause the food to deteriorate during drying and storage. Steam blanching is preferred over water blanching because it preserves more vitamins (figs. 198 to 200).

Since blanching time varies with altitude, thickness of vegetable slices, and quantity blanched at one time, use the times listed in the chart that follows as a guideline. The vegetables should be partially cooked—tender to cut, but not quite done enough to eat.

To peel or not to peel? If vegetables are not peeled, the skins are tough when rehydrated. You must make this choice based on your personal preference.

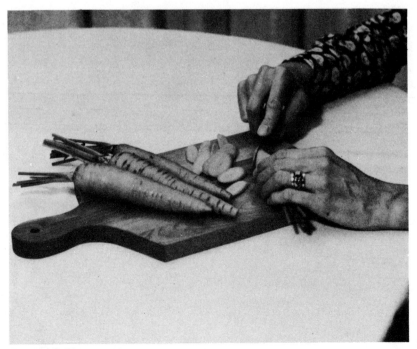

Fig.198. Cutting carrots

Fig.199. Putting carrots into kettle to steam

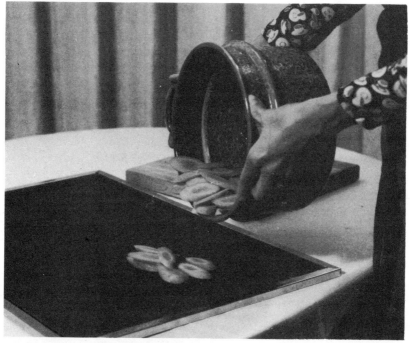

Fig.200. Pouring steamed carrots on tray

Fig.201. Putting frozen vegetables on rack

Frozen vegetables

If you want to dry vegetables the easiest way possible, buy commercially frozen ones and simply place them on dryer trays and dry them. They have already been blanched for freezing, so no other preparation is necessary. It works great for beans, peas, corn, carrots, hash brown potatoes, etc. (fig. 201).

REHYDRATING

When rehydrating vegetables, add just enough water to cover them. The time required may be from 15 minutes to 2 hours, depending on the type of vegetable and the thickness of the slices. Use the leftover water in sauces or soup to retain the most nutrients. Like fresh or frozen vegetables, they shouldn't be overcooked.

Many of the vegetables are best served dressed up with a sauce or used in soups or stews. See the chart on vegetables for "serving suggestions."

STORAGE

The storage life for vegetables is generally a little shorter than for fruits. Ideally, they should be used within 8 months to a year. Stronger vegetables should be used in 4 to 6 months. As with fruits, they should be stored in airtight containers in a cool, dry, dark place.

VEGETABLE	PREPARATION FOR DRYING	SERVING SUGGESTIONS
Green beans	Slice diagonally in 1″ pieces or French cut. Steam blanch 4 to 6 minutes.	Soups, stews, cream of mushroom soup.
Beets	Cook or steam until tender. Cut in ¼″ shoestring pieces.	Pickled beets: rehydrate with ½ cup water, ½ cup vinegar, 2 T. sugar, ½ tsp. salt, dash cloves, 1 bay leaf, 2 T. onion flakes.
Cabbage	Shred in ¼″ strips. Steam blanch 3 to 5 minutes.	Use in potato soup mix and stew.
Carrots	Peel, slice ¼″ thick, and steam blanch 3 to 5 minutes.	Soups, stews.
Celery	Slice diagonally ½″ thick. Steam blanch 2 to 3 minutes.	Soups, stews, powdered dry in blender for celery flakes or seasonings.
Chilies	Slice lengthwise or chop. Do not steam.	Powder dry in blender for chili.
Corn	Steam blanch on cob 3 to 4 minutes. Put in ice water. Cut from cob.	Rehydrate with 1 cup milk, 2 T. sugar, ¼ tsp. salt, enough water to cover.

199

VEGETABLE	PREPARATION FOR DRYING	SERVING SUGGESTIONS
Cucumbers	Slice 3/16″ thick and sprinkle with seasoning salt; dry until crisp.	Use as chip for dip.
Garlic	Peel cloves and slice in halves or thirds. Dry.	Powder dry in blender for seasoning.
Greens	Spinach, chard, etc. Steam until wilted; dry at 110°F. until crisp.	Powder dry in blender for soups.
Herbs	Leave on stems. Dry at 100° to 110°F. Remove from stems. Do not sun-dry.	
Mushrooms	Slice ¼″ thick lengthwise through the stem. Steam 3 to 4 minutes.	Stroganoff, gravy, chicken à la king, scrambled eggs, rice.
Okra	Slice pods ⅜″ thick crosswise. Steam 2 to 4 minutes.	"Gumbo soup"; dipped in cornmeal and fried.
Onions	Dice or slice lengthwise. Do not steam.	Chop dry in blender for onion flakes.
Parsnips	Peel and slice ¼″ thick. Steam blanch 3 to 4 minutes.	Soups, stews, or mashed with butter.

200

Peas	Shell. Steam blanch 3 to 4 minutes.	Soups, stews.
Peppers	Slice in ⅜″ slices or dice. Do not steam.	Soups, stews, scrambled eggs.
Potatoes	Peel, slice, steam blanch until translucent. Rinse in cold water.	Hashed browns, soups, stews.
Squash	Slice ⅜″ thick. Steam blanch 2 to 3 minutes. (Zucchini chips: prepare like cucumber chips.)	Soups, stews, with cheese sauce.
Tomatoes	Core and slice ⅜″. Dry until crisp.	Powder dry in blender. Soups or stews.

Jerky

Jerky is the name given to raw meat that has been sliced thin, seasoned, and dried. It is eaten dried and will not reconstitute when water is added. Home-dried jerky is far superior to commercial jerky and usually costs from $3 to $5 per pound compared to $12 to $18 per pound for commercial jerky. Four pounds of lean, fresh meat will make about 1 pound of jerky. Jerky was a staple in the diet of the pioneers and is still a popular food for camping and backpacking and is a nutritional snack for everyone.

Types of Meats to Use for Jerky

Any *lean* meat will make good jerky, but some cuts are better than others. Rump roasts, sirloin tip roasts, the round, and the brisket all make excellent jerky. Flank steak is so good that it has earned the reputation of being the "filet mignon" of jerky. Watch the meat specials in the store and try to get the best value.

It is also possible to use less expensive cuts of meat such as chuck roasts; but with the higher fat content, there is less jerky per pound of meat, and the jerky will not keep as long without freezing or refrigeration.

Fully cooked boneless ham may also be made into jerky, but must be stored in the freezer or refrigerator if you plan to keep it for more than a week or two.

Game meats make delicious jerky, but be sure to keep the meat clean and cold until ready to dry to avoid contamination or spoilage.

Preparation for drying

- Cut the meat across the grain in slices about 3/16-inch thick. The butcher will frequently cut the meat for you without additional charge. If you slice it yourself, partially freezing it makes it easier to slice evenly. Roasts are easier to slice and dry because you have larger pieces to work with.
- Remove excess fat.

202

- Marinate the sliced meat in one of the following recipes overnight in the refrigerator in a tightly covered container. You may also choose to smoke it if you have a meat and fish smoker, but I usually marinate it first.

Drying

Jerky should be dried at a temperature of 140° to 160°F. to prevent bacterial growth.
- Dry the jerky in single layers until a piece cracks but does not break in pieces when you bend it.
- As it dries, blot it with paper towels to remove any excess beads of oil that may collect on the top.
- Cut the jerky into smaller pieces with kitchen scissors and remove any visible fat.
- Let it cool and store it in an airtight container.

Marinade recipes

The following recipes are given for 2 pounds of sliced lean meat.

Spicy
2 tablespoons water
1 tablespoon A-1 steak sauce
1 tablespoon Worcestershire sauce
2 tablespoons soy sauce
½ teaspoon hickory-flavored liquid smoke
¼ teaspoon pepper
1 teaspoon salt
½ teaspoon onion powder
1 clove crushed garlic

Teriyaki
½ cup soy sauce
¼ cup brown sugar
1 teaspoon ground ginger
2 cloves crushed garlic
¼ teaspoon pepper

Hot 'n' Spicy
2 tablespoons water
2 tablespoons Worcestershire sauce
2 tablespoons A-1 steak sauce
½ teaspoon liquid smoke
¼ teaspoon pepper
1 teaspoon salt
¼ teaspoon cayenne
½ teaspoon onion powder
2 cloves crushed garlic

Sweet 'n' Sour
1 tablespoon soy sauce
½ cup vinegar
½ cup pineapple juice
⅓ cup brown sugar
¾ teaspoon salt
¼ teaspoon pepper
1 teaspoon onion powder
1 clove crushed garlic

Meats for Main Dishes

Home-dehydrated meats do not store well for long periods of time because of the high fat content; they become rancid after several weeks. However, meats may be dried and stored in the freezer until you're ready to take off on a trip and should keep well for a week or so.

Types of meat to dry

Lean beef, chicken, turkey, rabbit, fully cooked boneless ham, venison, and other lean game meats may all be dried.

Preparation for drying

- Fully cook the meat or poultry and remove any excess fat. It is also possible to use leftover meat that has been cooked to a tender state. Cut the meat into ½-inch cubes.
  Dry in an oven or dehydrator at 140° to 160°F. until crisp.

Storage

Store in airtight containers or plastic bags in the freezer until ready to use.

Reconstituting Dried Meats
Allow to soak in broth or bouillon until plump; cook with other ingredients.

RECIPES

To help you prepare foods ahead of time for your backpacking trek, or to inspire you to stop and cook a special treat once in a while, here are some suggestions.

Dried Fruit Goodies

Now that you have gone to all that work to dry fruit for your backpack, you'll want to make the most of the fruits you've dried. Here are some ideas for using them in recipes (fig. 202):

Dried apple/apricot balls

- Mix together
  1 cup finely chopped dried apricots
  1 cup finely chopped dried apples
  ¼ cup instant nonfat dried milk

Fig.202. Dried fruit goodies

- Mix and add to above   2 tablespoons orange juice
     ¾ teaspoon cinnamon
     2 tablespoons honey
     4 tablespoons Karo syrup

Roll into balls 1 inch in diameter. Roll in powdered sugar. Dry until firm at 140°F.

Apricot fudge

- In a heavy, 2-quart saucepan with buttered sides combine, heat to boiling, and cook to soft ball stage (238°F.) without stirring 1¼ cups granulated sugar
     1¼ cups firmly packed light brown sugar
     ⅓ cup whipping cream
     ⅓ cup milk
     2 tablespoons butter
- Remove from heat, cool to lukewarm (without stirring), and add   2 teaspoons vanilla

- Beat until candy thickens and loses gloss. Pour
  into pan after stirring in   ⅓ cup finely chopped apricots
                                     ⅓ cup finely chopped blanched
                                     almonds

Score into squares while still warm. When cool, cut into squares.

Apricot pegs

- Thoroughly mix together   1 cup finely chopped dried apricots
                                 1 tablespoon Karo syrup
                                 2 tablespoons honey
                                 1 tablespoon orange juice
                                 1 teaspoon lemon juice
                                 ⅓ cup unsweetened finely grated
                                 coconut

Knead, roll with hands into 4-inch "sticks," ¾" in diameter. Roll in coconut and dry in dryer 2 hours at 135°F.

Crunchy granola bar

- Stir together and warm in double boiler
                                 ½ cup crunchy peanut butter
                                 2 tablespoons honey
                                 1 teaspoon lemon juice
- Add and mix well   1¼ cups granola with dates

Either roll into balls or press into lightly greased 8x8-inch pan. Cut into squares after drying until firm in dryer or low oven (120°F.) with door open.

Mixed fruit balls

- Chop finely in blender or grind in meat grinder
                                 ½ cup raisins
                                 1 cup dates
                                 ¼ cup dried apricots
                                 ½ cup dried prunes

- Add and mix
  2 teaspoons lemon juice
  1 tablespoon Karo (white)
  1 tablespoon orange juice
  ¼ cup coconut
  4 tablespoons sunflower seeds
- Shape into balls and roll in
  ¾ cup finely chopped walnuts
  Dry in dryer until firm. Wrap individually in plastic wrap.

Granola with fruit

- Mix together
  4 cups oats
  1 cup coconut
  ⅓ cup sesame seeds
  1 cup wheat germ
  ½ cup sunflower seeds
  ¾ teaspoon cinnamon
  ½ cup rolled wheat
- Mix together and heat
  ½ cup honey
  ½ cup Karo syrup
  ½ cup brown sugar
  ½ teaspoon salt
  ⅓ cup orange juice
  ⅓ cup oil
- Add
  2 tablespoons vanilla
  Combine all ingredients. Bake at 200°F. until crisp.

- Add
  ½ cup raisins or dried cherries
  1 cup dried apples, apricots, or
  dates (chopped)

Bake 10 minutes longer.

Biscuit Mix and Variations

One of the greatest tastes in the out-of-doors is fresh-baked biscuits; dumplings and pancakes run them a close second. Here are some recipes for each.

Biscuit mix

- Stir until well mixed   8 cups sifted all-purpose flour
  1½ cups nonfat dry milk
  1 tablespoon salt
  ¼ cup baking powder
- Cut in and mix well   1½ cups shortening

Store in a tightly covered container in a cool place. The mix will last several weeks. Makes 10 cups.

Biscuits

- Add to   2 cups biscuit mix
- from   ⅓ to ½ cup water

Add enough of the water to the dry mix to make a dough that is soft but not sticky. Turn on a lightly floured surface. Roll or pat to ¾-inch thickness. Cut with a biscuit cutter, or cut into squares with a knife. Bake at 450°F. for 12 to 15 minutes.

Dumplings
- Mix well   2 cups biscuit mix
  ⅔ cup water

Drop by spoonfuls onto bubbling stew. Cook ten minutes uncovered and ten minutes covered. Place coals on lid of cooking container for best results.

Fruit dumplings

- Heat to bubbling   Your favorite dried fruit
- Mix together   2 cups biscuit mix
  ⅔ cup water

Drop biscuit dough by spoonfuls onto hot fruit. Boil gently 12 minutes without removing cover.

Pancake mix

- Put into a bowl

  1 cup biscuit mix
  1 egg
  ½ cup water

Stir just enough to mix. Dip spoonfuls onto a hot griddle. Turn when brown on griddle side and cook until brown on other side. Serve with syrup or preserves.

Potato-tomato scallop

- Combine

  Ham-flavored T.V.P.
  1 5½-ounce box scalloped potatoes and sauce mix
  2 envelopes instant tomato soup
  2 cups boiling water
  ¼ teaspoon oregano leaves

Simmer ingredients *slowly* until cooked (20 to 30 minutes).

Beef stew and dumplings

- Place into
- and let stand ten minutes

  4 cups boiling water
  4 teaspoons instant minced onion
  4 ounces freeze-dried beef cubes

- Into the meat stir and simmer until thickened

  1 package brown gravy mix
  1 package beef-flavored mushroom soup mix

- Stir in

  2 cups (8 ounces each) mixed vegetables, drained

Prepare dumpings from biscuit mix; drop by spoonfuls onto the stew and cook for 20 minutes, covered.

Hot cocoa mix

- Combine

  1⅓ cups instant nonfat dry milk
  ⅓ cup cocoa

210

2 tablespoons non-dairy creamer
(powdered)
½ cup sugar
dash salt

Store in airtight container. For each cup cocoa, add ¼ to ⅓ cup dry mix to 1 cup boiling water.

Potato pancakes

■ Mix together   2 cups finely grated raw potatoes
     ¼ cup water
     2 eggs, beaten
     ¼ cup biscuit mix
     1¼ teaspoons salt
■ Drop potato patties into   ¼″ hot oil

Turn potato patties after browning on one side. Brown on other side and serve.

Logan Bread (Backpacker's Special)

Method: Bake this one at home to take with you on your backpacking trip

Time: About 3 hours

■ Mix together in a large bowl   4 cups water
   3 cubes melted margarine (¾ pound)
   1⅓ cups honey
   2 cups molasses
   1½ cups sugar
■ Combine dry ingredients in   10 cups whole wheat flour
   another bowl   ½ cup powdered whole milk
   1 teaspoon salt
   2 teaspoons baking soda

Combine wet and dry ingredients.

■ Add   1 cup nuts (if desired)
   1 cup raisins

Bake bread in four bread pans. Bake uncovered for 1½ hours. Cover with foil and bake another 1½ hours.

This bread can be cut into pieces and wrapped in foil. It will keep for a long time.

AFTERWORD

After many years of camping and of teaching outdoor cooking in home economics, I was asked to write curriculum guides on outdoor cooking for other home-economics teachers. These guides, as part of my master's thesis at Brigham Young University, later developed into *Roughing It Easy.*

Since that time, as I have traveled, teaching and demonstrating these techniques, many people have shared their camping experiences and ideas with me.

As I have continued to enjoy the great outdoors, I have tried to use many of these ideas as well as create new ones to share with you in *Roughing It Easy 2.* A special thanks to all who in turn have shared their ideas with me.

I extend an open invitation to anyone who has additional outdoor ideas to send them to my publisher, Warner Books, 75 Rockefeller Plaza, New York, New York 10019.

Though this book has covered only a limited scope, both in car camping and lightweight camping, it would take volumes to include everything on the subject. I hope it has inspired you and will help bring many happy hours to you and your family.

If the book influences you to take a trip into nature and cook one meal (whether in foil over coals or in a skillet by solar heat), if it helps you to be more comfortable in camp for only one night, if it motivates you to dry only a few apricots in the sun for a backpacking trip, I will have received my reward for the painstaking work of gathering, testing, writing, rewriting, deleting, and adding to the ideas in this book. Happy camping to you!

ABOUT THE AUTHOR

Dian Thomas is the recipient of Utah's Outstanding Young Woman of the Year award for 1976 and is named in the 1976 edition of *Outstanding Young Women of America.*

Dian has distinguished herself in many ways since the days, a few years ago, when she was a kitchen helper at the Brighton, Utah, LDS (Mormon) camp for girls. From kitchen helper at the Brighton camp, Dian was promoted to counselor, then to director of the camp. She worked at the camp for seven years. She completed her undergraduate studies in home economics education at Brigham Young University. Her teaching career began with a junior high foods program where she introduced an outdoor cooking unit into the curriculum.

Dian was one of the first to pioneer outdoor cooking techniques as a part of a home economics curriculum. She went on to complete her master's degree at Brigham Young University and teach in the home economics department.

Her best-selling book, *Roughing It Easy,* was inspired by the combination of that experience and her camping background. *Roughing It Easy* was on the *New York Times* best-seller list for two months, climbing to the number two spot in that time. Its popularity resulted in its being featured as book of the month for Field and Stream Book Club. It is now being translated into several languages and printed in other countries.

Dian has lectured throughout the United States, Canada, Japan, and Mexico, has appeared on over 300 TV shows, and has had numerous newspaper and radio interviews. She has been on several national TV shows, including the Johnny Carson Show, the Mike Douglas Show, Good Morning America, To Tell the Truth, NBC News, and USA Productions. In Canada she has appeared on Canada A.M., the Alan Hamel Show, and Luncheon Date.

Forecast magazine presented Dian with a 1975 national service award in home economics education.

In spite of all these accomplishments and her busy schedule, Dian has time to reflect on her experience as a kitchen helper at the Brighton camp. She hopes those girls who camped with her then—and later when she was a counselor, then the director—caught the spirit of that outdoor adventure and went on, as she has, to reap the rewards that can come as the result of such an experience.

"Wizard of the Woods... In the world of summer soldiers and would-be woodsmen, Dian Thomas is a four-star general."—*Houston Chronicle.*

INDEX